# Planting
# Dandelions

# Planting Dandelions

## FIELD NOTES FROM A SEMI-DOMESTICATED LIFE

*Kyran Pittman*

RIVERHEAD BOOKS
*A member of Penguin Group (USA) Inc.*
New York
2011

RIVERHEAD BOOKS
Published by the Penguin Group
Penguin Group (USA) Inc., 375 Hudson Street, New York, New York 10014,
USA • Penguin Group (Canada), 90 Eglinton Avenue East, Suite 700, Toronto,
Ontario M4P 2Y3, Canada (a division of Pearson Penguin Canada Inc.) •
Penguin Books Ltd, 80 Strand, London WC2R 0RL, England • Penguin Ireland,
25 St Stephen's Green, Dublin 2, Ireland (a division of Penguin Books Ltd) •
Penguin Group (Australia), 250 Camberwell Road, Camberwell, Victoria 3124,
Australia (a division of Pearson Australia Group Pty Ltd) • Penguin Books India Pvt Ltd,
11 Community Centre, Panchsheel Park, New Delhi–110 017, India • Penguin
Group (NZ), 67 Apollo Drive, Rosedale, North Shore 0632, New Zealand (a division
of Pearson New Zealand Ltd) • Penguin Books (South Africa) (Pty) Ltd,
24 Sturdee Avenue, Rosebank, Johannesburg 2196, South Africa

Penguin Books Ltd, Registered Offices: 80 Strand, London WC2R 0RL, England

"Mommy Wears Prada" and portions of "For Richer or Poorer," "D-I-Y Spells DIE,"
"A Pilgrim's Progress," and "Feast of Sorrow" first appeared, in slightly different form,
in *Good Housekeeping*.

Library of Congress Cataloging-in-Publication Data
Pittman, Kyran.
Planting dandelions : field notes from a semi-domesticated life / Kyran Pittman.
p.      cm.
ISBN 978-1-59448-800-9
1. Motherhood.   2. Families.   3. Man-woman relationships.
I.  Title
HQ759.P548      2011                    2010048173
306.874'3092—dc22
[B]

Printed in the United States of America
1   3   5   7   9   10   8   6   4   2

BOOK DESIGN BY AMANDA DEWEY

*Penguin is committed to publishing works of quality and integrity.
In that spirit, we are proud to offer this book to our readers;
however, the story, the experiences, and the words
are the author's alone.*

*Dedicated to my mother, Marilee, who is my homeland;
to Patrick, who is my refuge; and to my sons—
Alden, Jonah, and Carey—a mighty nation.*

# Planting
# Dandelions

# Introduction

I jumped the white picket fence. Not in the way the story usually begins, with the heroine breaking out, busting loose, setting off across the wild world in search of her authentic, enlightened self. That would be uncharacteristically normal of me. I broke in, not out.

Some people need to break out. They're called to distant, exotic places to find truth and wisdom: a monastery on a mountain top, a boat on the high seas, the foot of a bodhi tree. There's nothing wrong with that. I happened to be called to find it in the laundry room and in Cub Scout den meetings. That's what I get for following *my* bliss. But those are exotic locations to me.

My children laugh when I tell them Mommy's an alien. "Look, it says so right here," I say, showing them my United States permanent resident card. To them, "alien" conjures images of E.T., the extraterrestrial being trying to navigate suburbia, *Sesame Street*, and trick-or-treat. It's more apt than they know. I came from "out there." Way out there. Fifteen years ago, I pushed off from a forgotten island at the edge of the continent and landed in middle America. I came to marriage from an adulterous, scorched-earth love affair. I went from being a wild child to being a good mother. I grew up in a home that was free-thinking, free-loving, and free-falling, and willingly entered a life of Cub Scouts on Monday, bills on Tuesday, playgroup on Wednesday, groceries on Thursday, errands on Friday, sex on Saturday, church on Sunday.

Some people come here automatically, to this town called Ordinary. The straight and narrow route will take you right to the middle of it in a hurry. Some people never know anything else. But I hitched in by the back roads, peered over the fence, and chose it.

I choose it every day.

"Beeeee good," I tell my sons, turning back to my field notes, the blog where for five years I've recorded my outside-looking-in observations on this big, little life. Part Underwood typewriter, part Moleskine journal, part refrigerator door; it's become a catchall for everything that digging in yields up.

"Look at this," I'd say, holding up some fragment of everyday to myself and anyone who happened to be reading, turning it over this way and that. *Look.*

People began wandering over to see what it was I was so taken with. First a few online readers, then more. Then *Good House-keeping* began to publish my essays, and the neighborhood suddenly got a whole lot bigger. "I have something just like that!" my virtual neighbors would say in a comment or an e-mail, and come running back holding the stories they found in their own backyard. They offer them up with a mix of shyness and excitement. Sometimes they doubt themselves.

I thought maybe it was worth something, but I don't know . . .

It's probably too small to matter . . .

It's kind of a mess and it's broken in places . . .

"It's beautiful," I tell them. It's funny. It's deep. It's *extraordinary*.

*Look.*

We live in an age that exalts lifestyle over life. We call caterers and decorators "gurus." Whole television networks are dedicated to telling us how our homes, gardens, tables, and wardrobes should look. Even our beliefs are subject to fashion—the more exotic, the better. But most people can afford only the extract—they get some of the flavor, but none of the substance. Imported spirituality is the new truffle oil.

I believe in seeking. I believe ardently that you should drop everything and run toward your true self, as far as you have to go. But I want to put in a word for the path that winds through the backyard, because it can be just as meaningful and wondrous as the one that goes up the mountaintop, if it's *your* path. You want a spiritual discipline? Try staying vitally connected to the same person year in, year out, through surprise pregnancies, late mortgage payments, toilet seat battles, and the occasional, strong temptation to walk away and make a living tending bar somewhere on the coast of Maine. Domestic life is full of moments of truth, if you stay awake to them.

What follow are some of my moments of truth. Writing them down is what keeps me awake and alive to that which is everyday and near. I hope they speak to the possibility of settling down without settling for, and the power of small things to make a life infinitely vast. They are an apronful of stories carried breathlessly up to the fence by that strange woman in town, me. They are for my neighbors who live inside the white picket fence with me, and they are for the wanderer who pulls off to the side of the road, looks over it, and wonders why anyone would want to live there.

Look. Look *what I found. Come see.*

1.

# The Hitch

**W**ill you marry me?" Patrick asked.

A light breeze came up, and the woods around us fidgeted; a whispered commotion among the fallen brown leaves. I opened my eyes and looked past bare branches of hickory and oak into the flawless February sky. It was my first winter in the South, and it felt more like early autumn to me, just crisp enough to wear a sweater. The sun had warmed the sandstone ledge we'd chosen for our picnic, and the trail that ran beside it, winding through a picturesque Arkansas valley, seemed reserved for our private enjoyment. It was a perfect day.

So why did he have to go and ruin it with that question?

Fortunately, I had an easy out. A wee technical glitch: I was already married to someone else.

That wasn't part of the official story we gave when people

wanted to know how on earth a guy from Arkansas and a girl from Newfoundland came to meet. Nor was the manner of our introduction. "We met in Toronto," we'd say, as if we'd both had other business there, besides meeting in person for the first time, after three months of writing torrid and anguished e-mails. It's quaint to think such a thing was once unheard-of, but for years we thought if word got out that we met on the Internet, we'd wind up on some lurid afternoon talk show.

"It's a long story," we'd say, if someone should press for details. "It's complicated."

But it wasn't, not really.

Two people fell in love. What other story is there?

Granted, I hadn't seen my husband in nearly twelve months, but I made the case—prim adulteress that I was—that it wouldn't be *proper* to get engaged.

"Ask me again when I'm free," I said lightly. It was ridiculous. I had never been *more* free. I had run away from home. I had no job. Patrick supported us both with his salary as an art director for a small ad agency, the one place in town that would hire him after he threw his career and professional reputation down the drain, chasing me up and down the North American continent for a year. I spent my days doing pretty much whatever I felt like. Once a month, I showed up to read a few poems at an open-mike session held in the back of a downtown bar, and that was as close as I wanted to come to having a commitment.

I left responsibilities and routines behind with my wedding china and crystal, part of the scaffolding that had propped up my married life. It was a shelter I'd constructed from scraps of conventional wisdom, papered over with pretty magazine pictures, and glued together with sheer wishful thinking. When I met Patrick, it all came down in a jumbled heap. Suddenly, none of it made the slightest bit of sense to me. I didn't know why I was dressing for success, or saving for retirement, or drinking enough water, or not going to bed angry. I stopped working, planning, and counting. I slept too little, drank too much, took up smoking. Why not? My whole life was on fire.

I stayed in the smoldering ruins for a while, too sad and too scared to move on. Then I left, bringing my sadness with me because it was familiar by then, like the smell inside my husband's raincoat, which I kept, also—as if I needed it in the high desert of central Mexico where Patrick waited. A few months of sun and alcohol drew the dampness from my soul. By the time our money ran out, I was ready to resurface. We headed back across the border to the United States, where I began to enthusiastically embrace life, liberty, and the pursuit of happiness.

I was carefree, and altogether careless. Earlier that winter, I'd gone with some girlfriends on a weekend road trip to Dallas, hell-bent for leather, with no thought for what might happen to me if we got pulled over on the interstate, somebody's joint in the ashtray, a temporary visitor stamp in my passport. In a tattoo parlor in the nightclub district known as Deep Ellum, I got my navel pierced.

"You're bleeding a lot," the guy who skewered me remarked. "Been drinking much this weekend?"

I'm in a tattoo parlor in Deep Ellum on Sunday morning, getting a hole bored through my belly button, I thought. He needs to ask if I've been drinking?

When I arrived back at our apartment—hours late, clutching a bloody gauze pad to my stomach—Patrick took one look and assumed I'd been mugged and stabbed. Even after I calmed him down, he was less than titillated by my antics. He had been glad to see me throw off the pall of guilt and grief, but he was beginning to consider the tiger and its tail. What spurred his proposal, several rocky weeks later, was the fear that he was losing me. In my experience, one of three suggestions almost always gets floated as a life preserver whenever a serious relationship starts to founder: get married, have a baby, or buy real estate together. Any one of those propositions is challenging enough under ideal circumstances, but that rarely stops people from thinking that the solution to an already complicated situation might be to make it more so. I was sure Patrick's sudden desire to get engaged sprang from the same last ditch as my estranged husband's insistence that we should start thinking about having children, just before we finally split up.

"You'd be a bad mother anyway," he shot at me, when I couldn't agree that babies were a priority. It was in those last bitter days when he would throw any words that would cut me, and I let him, because I absolutely deserved it, even when he hurled his scotch glass across the room in blind frustration one night, aiming for the wall, and it broke across my forehead instead, to his grief and horror.

It was a very small cut, but the physical pain was a relief. Here, at last, was a feeling that was simple, direct, and honest. I didn't want it to go away. The throbbing spot on my temple was the nearest thing to lucidity I had felt in a long time. We stooped together to pick up the bits of broken glass, our heads bowed, as if in prayer, over what was shattered and couldn't be put back together; the awful mess I'd made. He was a gentle and kind man who adored me, and I was making him crazy, because I had fallen in love with someone else, and I could not let either man go. I was a bad wife. Of course I would be a bad mother.

Patrick, looking from the outside in, took my part when I wouldn't, gallant as only the interloper can afford to be. But now the triangle had turned, and he found himself in my husband's former corner, while a poet I'd met at the open mike occupied his. I told myself it wasn't cheating. Or if it was, it was covered by my preexisting state of adultery, and I could just slip it in under general faithlessness. I rationalized that my relationship with Patrick was elastic and expansive enough to handle me testing my wingspan. But even as I raced breathlessly from "meeting" to "meeting" with my poet friend, even as we kissed hungrily, backed up against a table strewn with the drafts of our poems we were ostensibly "meeting" over, I knew I was being stupid. I'd used up all my allowable karmic tax deductions where cheating was concerned. To keep repeating the lesson was to be willfully remedial. The piercing in Deep Ellum was my attempt to snap out of it. I needed to get lucid.

The poet had his own reasons to not be stupid. When I came back from Dallas, we agreed to end it before the furtive make-out sessions went any further and things got out of hand, a distinction I had yet to demonstrate any aptitude for making. I was barely through patting myself on the back when Patrick found out about it anyway.

It was one thing for me to decide it was over between me and the poet. Being told it was over was another. After all, Patrick was the one who had come along and busted open my pretty, safe life, insisting I deserved to be free. Who was he to shut the gate now? Maybe it was over, and maybe it wasn't. We fought about it for weeks. He wanted a promise of fidelity, and I didn't want one more thing in my life that could get broken. But then he smashed his three-thousand-dollar Martin guitar into a tinder pile of splinters and unlashed strings, to illustrate the point his words weren't driving home: something had gotten broken anyway. The guitar was the only object of value he'd kept through our cataclysmic affair, which had cost him his house, his job, and his savings. It was the last thing he had left to sacrifice, the final installment of my ransom, and he was ready to walk away.

It was a repeat performance of a one-act melodrama. New man, different props, same me. I was tired of driving nice guys crazy. I was a bull, and all the world a china shop.

I knew I had to assume some responsibility for my life and for my relationships. I decided to take another stab at monogamy. I was even willing to find a job, if it would keep me busy and out of trouble. The risk of idleness was worse than the threat of deportation, so I put the word out among our drinking associates that I was looking for work. Our drummer friend, Hollywood, a weathered and whiskered reprobate in the mold of Levon Helm, sent me to a blues shack down by the tracks, the venerable Whitewater Tavern.

As far as anyone knows, the Whitewater has been in Little Rock longer than Jesus, and its "corner crew," the shift of hardcore regulars who cling to the corner of the bar with the tenacity and devotion of old-world Catholics at daily Mass, sprang out of the red dirt with it. Its hymnal is the blues. Hang around awhile and you will hear "Stormy Monday" in more variations than should be musically possible or musically desirable. The place cycles through phases of vogue. Every few years, a new generation of white college kids rediscovers it, and it becomes the fashionable place to demonstrate one's authenticity and hipster cred. New management comes in with new ideas. "Stormy Monday" goes out, replaced by punk, or pop, or rap, or whatever music the hot new band in town is playing. The corner crew hunkers down; smokes, drinks, waits. The band gets signed and goes on tour, the kids move on, the band breaks up, the place burns down. Somebody plays "Stormy Monday." Repeat. The Whitewater Tavern *is* the blues.

The trough between "kids move on" and "place burns down" was where I came in.

"I may be from southeast Arkansas, and I may talk slow. But that don't make me no *dumbass*."

Roy, the man who hired and trained me, had a point. Depending on who you asked, and how you defined it, he and his business partner—also named Roy—may or may not have been a couple of dumbasses, but no one could blame it on geography if they were. The term "good ole boys" may have originated in the South, but the South doesn't have a monopoly on the type. I was perfectly at home with the Roys. The mill town I grew up in was full of guys like them, country boys who swaggered into the city with grandiose plans and dodgy schemes. True, Roy did talk excruciatingly slow, but his drawl actually made him seem a little more refined. With a face as broken as a sailor's, and the body of a roughneck, he came across as brutish until he opened his mouth to speak in that deep Delta accent, the lazy beat of a cat's tail as its metronome. It was rumored that they had done all right for themselves in certain cottage industries, and were in the bar business to branch out. I made it my business not to know.

They hired me on as a cocktail waitress, essentially working for tips. My belly-button ring was investment attire. I worked in low-slung, bell-bottom jeans, with a halter top knotted at my bosom, and towering platform heels. My hair, formerly styled in a preppy bob, had grown long past my shoulders. There was no trace of the earnest young woman who had played dress-up in pencil skirts and blazers and toted a briefcase up and down the elevator to a job at the Board of Trade, just two years earlier. This work felt more real, and in a way, more respectable. The correlation between the effort I put out and the cash in my back pocket was direct and immediate. I had to hustle.

"Hold it HIGH," Roy bellowed at me, a cigar held askew between his teeth, my first night on the floor.

He gestured to the tray of drinks I clutched at waist level, and mimed the proper technique with one huge paw fully extended over his head, palm open to the ceiling and fingers spread. It seemed counterintuitive, but he was right. The tray was much easier to balance that way. I got the hang of it pretty quickly, along with other tricks of my new trade. Some were taught to me, like how to mix a perfect dry martini by chilling the glass with a shot of vermouth on ice, then dumping it out and pouring the gin or vodka over the trace that remained. Other skills I figured out on my own, like at what intervals a shot of whiskey would give me my second, third, and fourth wind without slowing me down. I was a good waitress, though I had a hard time counting American money in the dark, since it's all the same color. Customers must have wondered if my impairment was mental or visual, as I held each bill up to my eyes to read what value was printed on it before giving them their change.

Patrick took up a regular position at the bar, becoming a kind of staff stringer, helping out at the door and with closing before we took off for the after-hours clubs. Sometimes inventory had to be bought out of cash receipts. The Roys handed a wad of bills to him one night and sent him down to the nearest liquor store with a list. It was a rough neighborhood, so they gave him a pistol.

"Better take this," they told him.

"For what?" I asked, furious when I found out, "for someone to shoot you with?"

I had sidled up to the wild side, but in my mind, there was a line, and illegally carrying a gun crossed it. Partaking in the endless buffet of meth and cocaine crossed it. Too much booze crossed it. I didn't want my wings clipped, but neither did I want to crash and burn from flying too high. The Whitewater was full of addicts and fugitives with one demon or another at their backs. That wasn't free living, any more than a life of rigid convention was. The corner crew was looking less colorful and more tragic to me with each shift. It had been fun, but I couldn't avoid real commitments and responsibilities indefinitely. Except that I saw that I might, and that scared me more than all the guns, drugs, and booze put together. It was closing time.

Patrick had been content to let his knee-jerk marriage proposal drop, once I decided to consolidate my attentions. We were very happy together, and I didn't see how a piece of paper could add anything to our relationship, but I was in danger of wearing out my welcome with the U.S. government. I may have been an adulterous whore, but I was still too much of a nice Canadian girl at heart to stomach the life of an illegal.

I held out hope that my estranged husband would file for divorce from Canada, where it would be automatically granted after we'd lived apart for a year, but it was no surprise when the anniversary of our separation agreement came and went with no decree. We spoke once by telephone when I was in Mexico, long enough to know he wasn't inclined to do me any favors. It was time for me to go home and dispose of the remains. I flew back by myself to handle it.

In a courtroom I testified that yes, those were our names on the petition. Yes, we were married. Yes, we still lived separate and apart. It was our wedding ceremony in negative, the bride attended by absences. No dearly beloved, no rings, no troth, no thee. Just me. Divorce granted. I wondered if I should call my ex-husband to let him know we had been unmarried that day, if that would be courteous or cruel. I got his voice mail, and left a message, telling him one more time how sorry I was.

I flew back to Little Rock, and we made plans to get married, quickly, quietly, and without fanfare. I thought we might do something a little offbeat, elope to Las Vegas, or a country wedding chapel. It would be a second marriage for both of us, Patrick having divorced the year before we met. It was only four years since my big white first wedding. I lost a year of my life to obsessing over stationery, orchids, and stemware patterns; sashayed down a red carpet on my father's arm, all my doubts bound and gagged with a white satin bow. I suppose I thought if it looked like a fairy tale, it would end like one. I spared scant consideration for what came *after* happily ever after.

This time was different. I loved Patrick, he loved me, and that was enough. We didn't need to decorate it. But since he had proposed once to me already, I thought it would be nice to return the compliment, so I surprised him with a ring. He accepted it, but popped his own question again anyway before giving me my engagement ring, a deep green tourmaline for a stone instead of a diamond. Suddenly, we were engaged twice. Ironic, for a couple who'd insisted all along that we didn't need a ring.

From there, things took on a life of their own, as weddings

seem to do. As news spread up and down the bar that we were getting married, our nuptials turned into a barn-raiser. A guitar player with the house band mentioned that his wife was an ordained minister. We didn't care that she was ordained in the Church of Wicca, but we had to hide it from Patrick's Southern Baptist parents.

"What denomination did you say she was?" his mother kept asking.

"Ah, ecumenical something or other," we'd mumble, and then make up a burning question on floral arrangements or Italian buttercream, just to divert her attention.

As long as the Wiccan priestess was cool with the marriage license bureau, she was cool with us. Another band wife worked in the catering department of a posh hotel, and was able to swing us a deal on the fancy penthouse ballroom. Musician friends offered to come and jam for free beer. It was shaping up to be a party we couldn't stand to miss.

From my tip money, I bought a couple of yards of ivory charmeuse and a precious bit of silk Venetian lace. It was important to me that the materials were natural, and the dress simple. My previous wedding gown, hermetically entombed in a box in my mother's basement, was a white satin cyclone of sequins, netting, and bows. I was wary of sculpting another castle out of spun sugar. I wanted no artifice and a minimum of adornment. I sketched a long, plain slip with a small lace jacket, and brought it to our priestess, who, handily, also happened to be a seamstress. The result was even more spare than I had envisioned. I tried on the finished dress less than an hour before the ceremony, and discovered that the thin straps and low neckline didn't cover my bra, and that my underpants were clearly visible through the sheer fabric. Already running late for my own wedding, and faced with the prospect of going completely naked beneath handkerchief-ply silk, I dashed into the hotel gift shop, hoping in vain that they kept white G-strings and pasties on hand for spontaneous bachelor parties. There were only panty hose, queen size, in "suntan." I grabbed a pair and ducked into the lobby restroom to pull them on, hiking the waistband up to my armpits like a body stocking—ready to be lawfully wedded, for better or worse.

I told myself all along that it didn't really matter whether or not we got married; that I never really belonged inside the white picket fence. I'd jumped in, then jumped out, a trespasser. Unforgiven. It wasn't just that I'd betrayed my husband; more grievously, I'd betrayed myself, because I married him when I knew better. I had no faith in marriage, because I had broken faith. But then I found—through the writing of the vows, the choosing of the guests, the selection of the rings, and the countless other details, symbolic and practical—that it did matter. There was a gate in the fence that hadn't existed for me before, and it swung open as I walked up to it. Thus I entered matrimony, in full faith for the first time—soberly, advisedly, and in complete accordance with the purposes for which it was instituted. Wearing no panties and married by a witch.

# 2

# Meet the Sunshines

I'm too selfish to have kids," I told my mother a few years before my first child was born, sitting at a wrought-iron table, exhaling smoke and affecting world-weariness, like we were outside a café in Montparnasse and not an ice cream parlor in Hot Springs, Arkansas. I was baiting her, as daughters in their twenties do when mothers come visiting, but I secretly worried it was true. I was not very maternal as a child. The attention I gave to my dolls was erratic and occasionally catastrophic, like the time I fed Baby Alive mashed leftovers after the packets of synthetic baby food ran out. She became constipated and moldy, and eventually bugs hatched inside her motorized bowels. It was truly gross negligence. My Barbie dolls were just plain abused. I gave them garish makeovers with felt-tip markers, back-combed their long silken hair into frizzy blond Afros, and left them lying around naked, like skid-row floozies passed out on bathtub gin.

Then there was the Sunshine Family: Steve, Stephie, and their baby, Sweets. They were packaged as harmless, peace-loving hippies, but the constricted pupils in their vacant, round eyes suggested they might be a family the way the Mansons were a family. "Welcome to the warm world of The Sunshines," the back of the box said. Please leave your legal name and all your worldly attachments behind.

The Sunshines' world was not all that warm. According to my mother, who overheard me playing with them, Steve and Stephie were constantly bickering.

"Get the baby!"

"It's your turn!"

"I do everything!"

Poor Sweets. Poor Barbie, and poor, *poor* Baby Alive. If there had been a Department of Doll Social Services, they'd all have been taken away.

I got pregnant barely six months after I married Patrick. It was planned, but only for about five minutes in advance of conception. I had gone for a walk near the river and came back to our apartment with a four-leaf clover in my hand. I held it out to Patrick, and joked that it must be a sign, since it was Mother's Day, and thought I was probably ovulating. I was chronically forgetful about taking birth control pills. "There's a full moon tonight, too," I teased. "If we ever wanted to make a baby, now would be the time."

What Patrick heard was, "Let's have sex now."

I knew the moment we conceived. I knew in the same instant that I deeply wanted a baby. It seemed like a wish that was so new and tender called for some kind of reinforcement, so later that night, I made Patrick walk with me in the moonlight through a nearby wooded park, to an ancient oak, at the base of which I buried a little nautilus shell, an improvised symbol of protection for the tiny life I was sure flickered inside.

"This is pretty witchy," Patrick observed.

"It's asking a blessing," I said with authority, though I wasn't sure of whom we were asking it. I didn't believe in religion, but I was a poet, and I believed in its etymology, *religare*: to bind, to fasten. I was tethering a soul to my body. I whispered a prayer that our child would be blessed in every way, then we walked out of the woods, laughing and feeling high.

The next day, the signs seemed less clear. Maybe I was pregnant, but then again, why give up happy hour on the basis of hunches and superstition? It hardly seemed prudent. But I substituted sips of wine for swilling bourbon, and counted off the days before I could take a home pregnancy test and find out for sure. Fourteen days after the night of the full moon, I peed on a plastic stick, then watched with Patrick as the test developed. It was hardly the first time I'd nervously waited for the results of a pregnancy test, but this was a different kind of nervous. It was looking into the same little window from the opposite side.

The first pink line, and then the second, developed, confirming that I was indeed pregnant—and as far as I was concerned, the first woman in the history of the world to ever have been. It was critical that I gestate perfectly. I immediately regretted the couple of glasses of wine I'd had since conceiving. How bad was that, I wondered. Where else had I already gone wrong? I needed answers. I ran straight out and bought a copy of the prenatal health classic *What to Expect When You're Expecting,* commonly referred to as WTE within online pregnancy support groups—a convenient abbreviation, as it converts readily to WTF after you read the book.

What it told me to expect is that breeding is a highly complex and delicate process that requires standards and oversight not enforced in nuclear facilities. Fall short of 100 grams of protein a day, and you have only yourself to blame for your child's subpar intelligence. Allow preservatives or alcohol to cross the placenta, and you are begging for social and emotional disorders. Sugar? Why don't you just take a shit in the gene pool? It's the "Scared Straight" program of prenatal health.

We moved from our one-bedroom apartment into a two-bedroom downstairs duplex, and began scavenging yard sales for baby gear. The array of equipment deemed essential by parenting magazines was staggering. We couldn't hope to acquire all of it, even secondhand. The cost of raising a child to adulthood is a newswire perennial, with the bottom line always estimated to be roughly even with the GDP of a small developing nation. I take a skeptical view of the math today. It strikes me as a transparent scare tactic to keep poor people from reproducing, perpetuated by the same experts who would have it believed that a human fetus can't thrive if exposed to a Twinkie. But then, I believed every word. We *needed* that stuff.

Relax, said my midwives. Get some diapers and a car seat.

"How much will it all cost?" I fretted to Patrick.

"It will always cost a little more than we have," he said with uncanny foresight. "Relax."

The pregnancy books and magazines set impossible standards, but at least they were measurably impossible. I could tell where I came up short in grams of protein, or pairs of booties, and decide how much I was willing to worry about it. But I had no way of knowing if I possessed enough love or patience, or if I had the right psychological equipment on hand. I could avoid hazardous substances like preservatives and alcohol, but what about toxic feelings? Did anger, resentment, and insecurity cross the placenta? I hoped not, because I was surely exceeding the safe level. Angst churned in my gut like acid, and the source of it was the gaping disconnect between the way Patrick and I were experiencing pregnancy. It might seem like an obvious state of affairs, given that I was pregnant and he wasn't, but I had naively assumed that we would be of one mind, if not womb, from the moment of conception to the moment of birth. Meanwhile, he acted as if expecting a baby was just one of several compelling things going on in his life—sometimes as if it was the least of them.

I thought our rock-and-roll lifestyle was behind us, even before I got pregnant. When a kitchen fire shut down the bar I worked in, I heard it as last call, and decided to sign up with a temp agency and look for office work instead. Patrick, who already had a straight job, had been playing a little guitar on weekends with a rhythm-and-blues cover band, but it conveniently crashed and burned around the same time. Anyone could see the writing on the wall. But where I read "The End," he saw "To Be Continued," accepting a new gig with a band that had an aggressive practice and booking schedule, and an even more aggressive drinking schedule.

Years later, that band came up in a conversation at a dinner party. One of the women remembered seeing Patrick perform, but her husband was drawing a blank.

She nudged him. "It was the night we danced and danced, and then you threw up."

"That's the band!" Patrick and I said in unison. There was no mistaking it. Throwing up was a reliable identifier.

Gigs were a race between the band and fans to see who could get the most drunk first. Often as not, the band won, and the music suffered. The fans were never far enough behind to care. Patrick loved being onstage in front of an appreciative audience, even if they did tend to black out. He'd gone into his first marriage and a desk job straight out of art school, and it was a chance to trip down the path not taken. Only the path wasn't cut out for the wide load I was carrying. A year earlier, when I could drink, smoke, and party all night, I would have been fan number one. Instead, I was moody, tired, and stone-cold sober; number one shrew.

I was only a little bit sorry about begrudging Patrick his time with the band, but I was sincerely ashamed of resenting the other chief rival for his attention: his terminally ill mother. That spring, she had been diagnosed with late-stage cancer, and the life growing in me and the life slipping from her placed us at opposite doors of a long hallway, a juxtaposition that was cruel for everyone. Patrick's close-knit family was stricken with shock and dread, and I was deeply grieved with them, but I also felt cheated of our full measure of joy.

My mother-in-law was a classic southern matriarch, and I was just generically bossy. We were still negotiating which one of us was in charge of her youngest son's life when she fell ill. Cancer trumped me. I surrendered him, and hated myself for not being able to do so more graciously. He turned to the band to escape us both. I hoped she would use her leverage to make him quit, but she sighed and forgave him, which just made me feel meaner. I felt like the hysterical female in a Tennessee Williams play. I said terrible things to my husband. I wrote tear-stained apologies to the baby in my pregnancy diary for my poor choice in marriage, for the fighting and crying jags I was sure were poisoning the womb. Welcome to the warm world of the Sunshines.

I look at those entries now, and wonder what the hell I was thinking. I wouldn't give them to my son for a keepsake any more than I'd subject him to his birth video. That seemed like a necessary bit of documentation at the time, too, but I've since come to think we aren't supposed to witness our own primordial chaos. You can know too much.

Some of my underlying complaints about Patrick were justified, but all of it was hormonally amplified and distorted. It's true that his attentions were divided, but he was far from uninvolved. He came dutifully to doctor and midwife appointments, willingly attended birth class, and nodded appropriately as I read aloud from my books. But I wanted more than that. I wanted him in it with me. When I reproached him with that, he had no idea what I meant. "I am in it," he'd insist, "I couldn't be more in it." I'd dissolve into tears, because I didn't know what I meant either, except I felt terribly, unbearably alone, and none of the books told me to expect it.

Halfway through my term, I found a slim paperback tucked among the pregnancy and childbirth guides at the bookstore, called *Operating Instructions*. I could use a set of those, I thought, and took it home. When I came to the passage where Anne

Lamott described pregnancy as a "holy darkness," I wept with gratitude and relief. Now I knew. *This* was what to expect when you were expecting: the utter, unavoidable loneliness. Because no matter who's there standing by, pregnancy is a place you go all by yourself, just as my mother-in-law was going somewhere all by herself. Both of us moving deeper into the darkness, deeper into the holy. Not two doors to the hallway after all, but the same door, opening out and in.

I decided I wanted a home birth. People thought I was brave, if crazy, but the truth is, I fear and loathe hospitals. My only reservation was that our bedroom at home might be less than sterile.

"Compared to a hospital room?" the midwives asked. "Are you kidding? Just think about everything that's been on those beds and floors."

I preferred not to. I had a weak stomach when it came to things that oozed, spewed, or were extruded from other people's body cavities. So much so, I could hardly utter the words "snot," "puke," "poop." I hoped I'd be inured to my own baby's bodily emissions, but I seriously worried I might not. I had way more confidence in my ability to handle labor pains than I did in controlling my gag reflex during a diaper change.

The first signs that I might not be cut out for the sensory reality of motherhood went back as far as my sister Emily's birth in 1973, when I was four. Throughout my mom's pregnancy, I'd been led to believe I was getting a real live doll to play with on demand. When the baby came home, and wasn't immediately turned over to me, I felt robbed, like an expectant adoptive parent whose surrogate had, at the last minute, changed her mind. One early morning, when I heard Emily stirring in her crib before our parents were up, I decided to go claim that which was supposed to have been mine.

I crept in, and hoisted her out of her crib.

"I've got you," I reassured my sister, who smiled at me with total confidence. *My* baby. "I've got you now."

I set her on my hip, expertly. From here, there was nothing I couldn't handle. I would dress her, take her downstairs, get her breakfast, raise her to adulthood. Our parents could sleep for a hundred years. I was the mommy now.

Something smelled bad.

"I've got to change your diaper," I told her. I'd seen it done a hundred times. How hard could it be? You unsnapped her pajamas, pulled this tape away here, and that tape away over there, and . . . *ewww.* I left her for my mother to find.

As a little girl, I assumed I would grow up and have babies someday, but I saw them as accessories. Motherhood was a "look," like superstar or beach bunny was for Barbie. I pictured myself as a glamorous mother, a swish of skirts and a cloud of perfume, benevolent but remote. When I watched *The Sound of Music,* I rooted for the elegant Baroness, not goofy Maria, who was warm and funny like my own mother. My imaginary adoring children didn't have runny noses, or stinky diapers, or heaven forbid, throw up, as my sister did anytime she rode in a car for more than fifteen minutes. Whenever her motion sickness forced us to pull over, I slid to the window farthest away from her and covered my ears, but retched anyway, just from the idea of it. Particles of dry vomit were permanently embedded in the fake weave of the vinyl that covered the backseat of our Volkswagen

Beetle, and when the summer sun warmed it, a faint sour smell was released that nauseated me. My stomach hadn't strengthened with age. What was going to happen when my own baby vomited? How was I supposed to care for him if it made me gag myself? I hoped that evolution had it covered.

It did, not only through the provision of a bonding instinct that overrides squeamishness, but through the act of birth, so messy it leaves the mother no room to wrinkle her nose afterward at the natural bodily functions of the person who emerged through it. Patrick assumed—mistakenly—that the amnesty also extended to him. A few days after I delivered our son while squatting naked on our bedroom floor in front of him and three midwives, he cheerfully ventured to say that he supposed we could now dispense with the need for personal modesty, and ease my strict prohibitions on sharing the bathroom.

"Not on your life," I growled. "Get out."

It's pretty much impossible to describe the experience of falling in love with your child without sounding like a dope. I once showed up late for a college party where everybody was already tripping on magic mushrooms, and they were all compelled to provide me with running commentary on their altered state, which consisted mainly of profundities like *"Wow."* I couldn't get out of there fast enough. I know it's got to be as tedious to endure someone like me going on about how having children changes—no, *really changes*—everything.

I expected to love my baby, of course, but I didn't know it

would be crazy, over-the-moon, in-love love, the kind that turns every song on the radio into a dedication. I wept the first time I heard Aretha Franklin sing "Natural Woman" after I become a mother. My soul, too, must have been in the lost and found, I thought, to feel so redeemed. "Heaven, I'm in heaven," I crooned, as I danced him cheek to cheek around the house, to Fred Astaire. At nap time I gazed deep into his eyes, and held his little starfish hands, and was love struck. I was the crazy girlfriend who watches her man at night while he sleeps. If my son had had to withstand the full intensity of my adoring focus for the rest of his childhood, it probably would have screwed him up badly, but I was pregnant with his brother the following year.

The circumstances around that conception were considerably less dramatic than the first—there were no signs that time, unless you consider Saturday-morning cartoons a sign. We considered it an opportunity, and seized it. A few weeks later, the stick displayed the international litmus sign for "Told you so." Our second son was born two years and four days after our first. How the third got past us, we still aren't sure, but he arrived the year before the oldest started kindergarten. In a little over five years, I gave birth to three children.

At my high school reunion, a classmate told me that she'd heard about the first baby, and assumed it happened by accident. She couldn't believe I'd gone on to have two more. "No offense," she said, blatantly astonished, "but I never saw you as the maternal type."

I laughed, and told her no one was more surprised than than I was. She'd be even more astonished to see me with my kids. In spite of all expectations to the contrary, I am a good mother. Having easygoing children helps. Paradoxically, so do those same low expectations. In a culture that makes impossible demands of mothers, they've served to my psychological advantage. I figure I'm doing all right as long as I keep my babies free of mold and bugs. Everything exceeding that standard can be regarded as a personal triumph; success building on success. My boys flourish and thrive, and know they are beloved. If they are occasionally without clean socks, they understand it is a failure of planning, not feeling.

I still don't think of myself as "the maternal type." I like children in general, and love some in particular, but I don't want to mother any but my own. I don't beg to hold new babies, like some of my friends do, though I will cheerfully hold my arms out to receive one, if asked. But it doesn't naturally occur to me to shake baby feet, smell baby heads, or talk baby talk. I was initially taken aback when other women expressed those urges toward my baby. The first time a stranger came up and smelled my son's head, I thought she was nuts. We were at a party, back in the days when we just had one baby and were the people who took the baby everywhere. All the women wanted to hold him, and this one practically inhaled him.

"It's been years, but it's like I can feel my milk letting down," she gushed.

I was revolted. Not by her phantom milk production, but by the idea that this stranger was responding physically to my baby. I snatched him back, violated, as if I'd just seen her shove her tongue in my husband's mouth. I regarded it as an attempt at possession. Smelling is acquisitive. The sweet breast-milk smell of my newborn was mine. The smell of my sons' salty necks when they are bent reading and I crane in to kiss them, that's mine. The smell, layered and tannic, of the inside of my husband's robe when I pick it up off the bed in the morning: mine.

All mine.

I spoke a half-truth to my mother that day outside the ice cream parlor. I am selfish. But as it turns out, that's a good thing. It's easy to give the best of me to mine.

# 3

# Attach and Release

L et me get your number," I said to the woman as the dinner party came to a close. We had been discussing additives in food, and I was interested in hearing more of what she had to say about it. She obviously knew her way around a nutritional information label. I fumbled through my diaper bag for paper and a pen, and came up with a crayon. She handed me a small card.

"Thanks," I said, automatically flipping it over to the blank side, crayon poised. "Now, what was that number?"

She looked at me strangely. Then reached out and turned the card back over.

"It's printed on the card," she said. "Right there."

I stared at it in wonder. So it was. Along with her name, title, and place of employment.

"I remember these!" I blurted, like a demented person having a lucid breakthrough. "I used to have boxes of them. With *my* name on them."

She extricated herself while I was still studying the card, lost in reverie, as words like "memo" and "payroll" breached my consciousness. Words in a language I spoke once, but had not used in years and had all but forgotten. Cubicle. Break room. Boardroom. Stamps on an old passport buried deep in a drawer.

I never did call her. She was, according to the embossed lettering on her card, a degreed professional with a job title, an office, and regular working hours. I was a baby-wearing, co-sleeping, breast-feeding new mother; in essence, a marsupial. She probably took a shower every morning and put jewelry on before going to work. I was dressed for success if I could uncover a nipple in less than a minute. She had children who slept through the night and went to school during the day. From where I stood, that sounded like an urban legend, something I heard happened, but not to anyone I knew personally. Getting together would require us to project the movement of our days and plot a future point in time where our lives would intersect again, like astronomers predicting the next eclipse. I didn't see it happening for at least ten years.

I was then, and am still, for lack of a better word, a stay-at-home mom. I didn't intend to be. That wasn't what little girls who grew up watching *Mary Tyler Moore* were expected to become. I thought I would have a career. If I had a baby, I would take maternity leave and resume my career once that project was launched and running smoothly. But that idea was based on maternity benefits as they existed in Canada, and children as they existed in my mind. Having real children, in the United States, was a different proposition. There was no career to interrupt or resume. I barely got my U.S. work permit before I got pregnant, and then I worked temp jobs, none of which came with benefits or paid enough to make day care worthwhile. Even if I had a permanent position that paid well, I couldn't wrap my head around the meager American maternity leave of six weeks. It takes me that long after having a baby just to start thinking about personal hygiene again. The notion of myself as a briefcase-carrying mom, with a steady salary and a freezer full of breast milk, was the first of many maternal illusions I'd come to forsake, and probably the easiest one to let go. I was a college dropout who had always been able to talk my way into jobs that exceeded my education and maturity. But with no degree, and a foreign résumé, I was going to have to move my marker back to start. I was just as glad to sit out.

Patrick's paycheck covered our car payment and the rent and utilities for a two-bedroom apartment. Being at home afforded me the time to be creative with our resources and frugal with our money. I breast-fed and cloth-diapered, shopped with coupons, and cooked in batches. I studied parenting and nutrition books, joined Internet forums, and went to La Leche League meetings. I threw myself into domesticity with reckless abandon. I was zealous, idealistic, and probably quite tiresome, but it takes a certain fervor to get through the baby years. It helps to fall in love with your captors. The infatuation anesthetized the pain of separation from the person I was before: rested, unfettered, accessorized.

Some new parents struggle with abandoning normal. They wait for its return like castaways watching for smoke on the horizon; go slowly mad waiting for sleep, sex, and privacy to come back for them. I found it easier to face facts. Normal wasn't coming back. I moved deep into the interior of mothering, and forgot I'd ever known anything else.

Human beings have been keeping infants and young children within arm's reach ever since we had fur they could cling to. But in twenty-first-century middle America, that tradition is considered an alternative lifestyle. Fortunately, even in the suburbs, there is subculture, and it didn't take long to find kindred oddballs. Wearing a baby sling in public is like going out in a Highland kilt. It identifies you to your clan. I was taken in, and embraced, by a small tribe of mothers gathered under the umbrella of attachment parenting, a name popularized by Dr. William Sears's *Baby Book*. We met for weekly playgroup and monthly potlucks, and I looked forward to those times with an eagerness formerly reserved for romantic rendezvous. I was twenty-nine years old, and though I thought of myself as a feminist, and had grown up with a loving mother and sister, two splendid grandmothers, an abundance of aunts, and assorted female elders, for the first time in my life, I fell in head over heels in love with women.

How could I not? These were smart, passionate, funny, and fiercely independent women. Some were young moms, barely out of their teens, with tattoos and piercings; and some were routinely mistaken for grandmothers. There were those with advanced degrees and impressive résumés; and there were those who had become mothers before they had a chance to try their hand at anything else. Some were transplants, like me, and some had never left their hometown. They were all very brave. It takes guts to trust your own authority in the face of disapproval—and sometimes, harsh judgment—from doctors, relatives, and total strangers. Even within the group, eyebrows were sometimes raised at the mothers who were furthest off the grid: breast-feeding not just through but past toddlerhood; adopting controversial positions on education; or taking the concept of natural parenting to such an extreme that their kids were half feral and terrified all the rest. But our experience was common at the core, if not at the fringes. We could sympathize with each other's sleepless nights, aching backs, and cracked nipples without feeling defensive. We could joke about not being able to pry our attached kids off our bodies, and laugh at our mothers' concern that we were having sex next to our babies in the family bed. As if we were having sex, we said. We laughed harder at that, and then we cried. We reminded each other, over and over, that it was all such a short, sweet time; that our children would one day wean from our breasts, sleep through the night, and be independent. We were raising a healthy, emotionally intelligent, free-thinking generation to be a light to the world. We were all on the same mission, mothers-in-arms. I'm not going to pretend it was a utopian matriarchy. It wasn't. We could be unkind, sanctimonious, and petulant. But it was a sisterhood. And to me, it was oxygen.

Identifying myself as part of a movement not only provided me with an instant community, it made it seem like I had a plan. I adopted it like a new religion, with all the proselytizing and intolerance of the recently saved. I didn't just disagree with formula-feedings, disposable diapers, day care, and baby-schedulers, I had contempt for them. I pretended compassion for parents who were at their wits' end, but I really thought those who spanked and made babies cry themselves to sleep were child abusers. Yes, I was that asshole. I didn't make allowances for circumstances other than mine. I secretly judged working mothers for choosing a paycheck over the emotional well-being of their child. I conveniently forgot that I needed help learning to breast-feed at first, and had been lucky to have a midwife who could guide me. Those who chose not to nurse had to be uncaring or ignorant, and those who quit hadn't tried hard enough, obviously. It was difficult to fathom how other people could have their priorities so backward. I was both baffled and irritated when I was told by a neighbor, "You have to get away from your baby sometimes."

Why, I wondered, cradling my tiny son in his sling. He'd grow up and go away from me soon enough, perhaps as far away from me as I was from my own mother. Why in the world would I want to get away from him now, when he most wanted to be with me?

There would be plenty of time to take care of myself and my marriage later, I thought. If I noticed that some of the most fiercely attached mothers had spouses who seemed oddly *detached*, I didn't connect it with the intense focus on child rearing, or to my own marital health. Everything was secondary to my way and truth.

It must be said, before anyone glares hard and long on my account at the next mother they see nursing a toddler (who is probably getting enough evil looks as it is, and could use a smile instead), that my views weren't representative of the Order of the Sling. Some of us rode in on higher horses than others, and even the most evangelical among us was sure to have a counterpart on the other side of the playground, thinking we should all be arrested for indecent exposure of our breasts, and for endangering our children by sleeping with them. Moms are so hard on each other because we're so damn hard on ourselves. None of us can really be sure we're doing the right thing, or know how it's all going to turn out. Today, I believe most parents—even the spankers—love their kids as much as I do, and are doing the best they can, like I do. But you couldn't tell me that back then.

With each child, I became more relaxed, or maybe I was just more exhausted. At any rate, I was less rigid in my views. I found it was possible to compromise, and still be a good mother; perhaps, a healthier person. My firstborn wouldn't take a bottle or pacifier, for instance, because I hadn't dared introduce one before the recommended time, lest dreaded nipple confusion impair his breast-feeding technique. It worked. He was *very clear* on the difference, and spat out every kind of artificial nipple I tried. I couldn't be away from him for more than an hour or two at a stretch. It was awful. I was discovering that I did need to get away from my baby sometimes, if just to go to the dentist.

"Do what you have to do," I said with a meaningful look, as I left him with one of my nursing friends one morning so I could keep an appointment. I was only half joking.

With the next baby, I wasn't taking any chances. As soon as he seemed to get the hang of nursing, I gave him a bottle. "This is a bottle," I told him. "And this is a breast. Questions?"

He had none.

I was prepared to give the third one a pacifier as soon as his head was all the way out. He generally had one in his mouth, one clipped to his shirt, and one tucked in my pocket on standby.

Over time, I found I needed to revisit more than just my position on feeding and soothing. Having a second child forced me to consider how long I could possibly keep pouring so much of myself out. I was starting to think I might not be the earth mother I wanted to be, any more than I was the executive mom I thought I would be. After the first two years of immersion, the romance of homemade yogurt and hand-sewn sock puppets began to wear thin, as did my self-esteem. The labor involved in taking care of small kids is menial and repetitive. You're cleaning up other people's body waste day after day. There's an aspect of it that works on your ego in a good way. It can be a humbling act of devotion. It can also make you feel like shit. My complete financial dependence on my husband was subtly corrosive, too. I began to feel as if I wasn't really qualified to do anything but mind children, keep house, sort the mail, and make appointments—tasks that translated to the bottom of the pay scale in the job market. It frightened me. What if Patrick dropped dead, and I had to provide? Where would I even begin?

On top of all that—or more truthfully, buried deep beneath it—I was getting bored. Potlucks and playgroups were my main social outlet, and they weren't enough. I called Patrick at the office to talk, and sometimes fight, several times a day. I poured my creative energy into projects that never got finished, problem-solving that didn't help anybody, and any other diversion I could put between myself and the dread truth that as much as I adored my children, I needed something more to feel fulfilled. But I couldn't admit it without a specific idea of what "more" might be. I needed a clear exit sign.

It came in the form of a part-time job as an assistant to a priest at the Episcopal church I had wandered into one Sunday when my firstborn was a few months old. I wasn't sure what I was doing there, but it intrigued as much as perplexed me, so I kept wandering back. The liturgy was familiar; the "smells and bells," as Anglicans say, of my Catholic schooling, minus the guilt and the gory crucified Jesuses. The service brought some structure to the week, when my days were so much like each other that it seemed to have no beginning or end. On Sundays, at least,

I had something to get up and get dressed for, a place to go. It was a portal to a world that included, but didn't revolve around, children. And it was a space where I had a chance to connect with myself, a prayer of hearing the small, still voice within— if the signal hadn't gone dark permanently. The priest, Susan, was a sexy, mature woman with a sleek silver bob and flowing purple batik robes—so radically different from the cadaverous Catholic priests I'd known as a kid, that I had to do a theological double-take. I was wary about the Jesus-y bits, but I was drawn to her offbeat book groups and workshops on meditation and dreams. It was in one of those that she mentioned she was losing her assistant.

The small, still voice pinged. *That's your job.*

I didn't say anything, but when she offered the position to me a few weeks later, I considered myself drafted. "Yes," I said, without really knowing what I was agreeing to do. It turned out to be the perfect part-time job for the next five years, requiring me to develop professional skills that went well beyond making appointments and sorting the mail. It alleviated my fear that my next résumé would have to include a section called "The Missing Years."

I enrolled the children in a half-day Mother's Day Out program, two days a week. They had hardly ever known a babysitter, so it felt like I was shipping them off to boarding school. Life was supposed to come through me before it came to them. It was my role to screen, diffuse, and manage their every experience. Nobody else, not even their father, was qualified enough, in my eyes. I planned to keep this up through the school years by educating them at home. Before any of my children could hold a crayon, I was already researching curriculums. One week I leaned toward the freestyle "un-school" approach to learning; the next I was sure that a classical education with Latin lessons was right for my future academy. Or we would mix it up, borrow from the best of both. I imagined us sitting around the dining room table, conjugating verbs and finger knitting, myself as a cross between Mary Poppins and the wizard Merlin—every lesson a magical adventure with talking animals and musical numbers.

I loved the idea of homeschooling. Still do. But I must have been thinking of someone else's home. My fantasy didn't account for the fact that I'd never been interested in teaching kids, or admit the possibility that there were trained teachers who had always wanted to teach kids, and might have something of value to offer mine. How could they? In my mind, motherhood was a kind of enclosed terrarium, a bell jar that contained everything my children would ever need to grow. I didn't realize how much bigger their lives—and mine—were going to get. Like the little boy in one of my old storybooks who buys a goldfish and has to keep finding larger containers to hold it, I've had to ditch one cherished idea of motherhood after the other for a more spacious one.

I was braced for every possible repercussion of placing the boys in day care, except that we all might like it. It was a revelation to pick up my two-year-old at the end of his day, and hear the pleasure in his voice at having news to tell me. It was bliss to have five hours to myself at a stretch. None of us were going to fit back under the jar. The third baby was on the wait list for Mother's Day Out *in utero*. They each graduated from a couple of days a week to half-days all week, then full days at school all week, and my work, like the contents of my purse, has tended to expand to fill all available pockets of space.

Along the way, I morphed from part-time priest assistant to full-time writer. I have a desk, but my "office" is generally the end of the dining room table. According to the amount of e-mail spam I get, advertising work-at-home opportunities for moms, I'm living the dream. It's not unlike the dream where you sit down for an exam and realize you have no pants on. Only the exam is a magazine deadline, and there's a chance that I really don't have any pants on. Every day is casual day at Work-at-Home-Mom Inc. Also, it's always bring-your-kid-to-work day, because my office hours don't neatly correspond with the ringing of the school bell. The kids come home around the same time of day that New York editors usually approach the bottom of their to-do lists, where my name and number sometimes happens to be.

The first time one of my essays was picked up for publication, I had to leave a voice mail for one of those editors, a person I aspired to work with again and upon whom I wished to impress a certain air of decorum and professionalism. That whole neurotic, hapless, flying-by-the-seat-of-my-pants, Wendy-Among-the-Lost-Boys thing? Ha-ha! Merely my literary persona, my dear. I can turn it on or off at will.

I left my message, and closed with this: "I have to go now. The baby is naked, and he has a hammer."

It could have been worse. On any other day that week, I could have instead closed with:

"I have to go. The baby is locked in the dog crate."

"I have to go. They are making a contest of jumping over the pee on the floor."

"I have to go. They just lassoed the ceiling fan."

I decided I needed the proverbial "room of one's own," so I claimed a utility room at the back of the house, which had previously been designated as an arts and crafts space for the kids, a place where mess-making was allowed. Of course they weren't the slightest bit interested in it until I moved a desk, a chair, and my laptop in and declared it off-limits.

I might as well have baited it with candy. A few weeks later, in the middle of a project, I walked into my sanctuary to find it completely trashed. A cupboard full of art and school supplies had been pillaged. Paint was splattered on the floor, my file folders and copy paper strewn across it, a fine dusting of craft glitter sprinkled over everything. I went looking for the perpetrators, half tempted to rub their noses in the spilled glitter, wondering if I ought not to have revised my position on spanking along with everything else. I apprehended the vandals in the driveway, making mud pies on an industrial scale from a batter of dirt, water, poster paints, and school glue. They stared at me like raccoons caught in headlights on the rim of a dumpster.

"For the love of God," I implored them, "go watch television."

At various junctures, I've tried again to establish a regular work space, as if I were a regular person with a regular job. I stake my claim, furnish it, and accessorize it with file folders, letter sorters, and Post-it notes. Somehow I always wind up right back at the dining room table, laptop propped open amid the dirty breakfast dishes and school papers. It seems that I'm resistant to a room of my own, maybe for the same reasons the boys weren't interested in a creative space that was designated exclusively for them. We like to be near each other. My sons' correct sense of their place in the middle of my life remains intact. The difference now is that they aren't expected to occupy the whole of it.

I never fell out of love with my mothers-in-arms. There are some I see regularly, though more often over dinner or a glass of wine than at the playground. These tend to be the moms who also sought the middle way, though I'm glad to know that others are still out there on the lonesome high road, if only as a challenge to conventional wisdom, an oxymoron if there ever was one. Every one of the rest of us has strayed from our early ideals in some way that would have appalled us then. We laugh and cry, and remind each other how short, how sweet, that time was.

As we assured each other would one day be the case, our children have, one after the other, weaned from our breasts, left our beds, learned to sleep through the night. On a Saturday morning, mine can get up, turn on the television, pour their own cereal, and fend for themselves until I've had my first pot of coffee. Before I'm done brewing the second, the screen door opens and bangs shut and the older two are gone, climbing fences, riding bikes, rounding up their neighbors, scheming sleepovers. Even the youngest can spend a whole night away from home now. They are on their way.

I still don't feel a pressing need to be apart from them for more than a day. Whenever I have to travel without them, the final hours approaching departure are filled with second thoughts. I regret the decision to go, procrastinate packing, scheme to get out of it. Anything could happen, I tell myself. Life is too short to spend one precious minute away from the ones I love. Why *should* I go?

Against the undertow of impending separation, I pull them closer, touch them more, hug them longer. I bring my face to their hair and breathe in like it's my last chance at oxygen for a thousand miles.

And then it's time. I force myself to push off, to remember who I am without them, so that when it is their turn to leave me, I'll still know.

4.

# D-I-Y Spells Die

O ne morning a year, I wake up and remember that tomorrow is Pinewood Derby Day, an annual Cub Scout event that requires Cubs to design, carve, and pimp a car from a hand-size block of wood, which is then raced on a state-of-the-art electronic track, run by grown men wearing neckerchiefs. Space shuttles are launched with less precision and intensity than Pinewood Derby cars. There are exacting restrictions on dimension and weight that come down to micro-units of measurement. There are legalities concerning exterior enhancements and the types of lubricants allowed on the axles. There are innumerable websites devoted to Pinewood Derby aerodynamics, but form is valued closely behind function, with prizes awarded for "Most Patriotic" design and "Most Creative." You can't pull a prizewinning

Pinewood Derby car out of your ass at the last minute, which is why our Cubs never win prizes. It's not their lack of competitiveness, it's their parents'. We are the seventies Chrysler of Pinewood auto production. Everyone else is racing Bugattis and our kids get K-cars.

I put Derby Day on the family calendar, and e-mail Patrick weekly reminders as the date nears, but somehow it always falls off his radar. When I go to him on Derby Eve and tell him there are twenty-four hours left before weigh-in, he acts like it's an ambush. In the interest of preserving the marital trust, I will enable the "mute" button on the scene that invariably follows. But if you were to write captions based on observing our body language and facial expressions, you might come up with something like this:

"Are you fucking crazy??"

"Are you??"

And that would more or less capture the gist of it.

Sometimes—most times—I think we are doing a pretty good job as parents. Our boys slept between us as infants. They were breast-fed into toddlerhood. They never had to cry longer than it took us to figure out what was needed, and answer the need. We may not always keep up with the Joneses, but they have bikes, books and bunk beds, soccer, school and Scouts, and most of the other privileges of being a middle-class kid in America. We work hard at being whole people in a healthy relationship. Most times, I think my kids are as lucky to have us as we are to have them.

But then we hit a bump and it derails me completely. Instead of feeling like we are doing an outstanding job, I wonder who thought it would be a good idea to give *us* three human beings to care for. We can't keep houseplants alive. We can't change light-bulbs. We can't sew badges on uniforms—hell, we can't remember to *wash* the uniforms—let alone remember the goddamn Pinewood Derby. Other people seem to have no problem at all with going to work, paying their bills, mowing their lawns, dusting their ceiling fans, painting their door frames, and returning their library books on time. What is wrong with us, I ask myself on days like that. Did we miss an orientation session on Living Life? Did we ride in on the short bus?

Homemaking is not my forte. Or my husband's. Even before we had our own junior demolition crew, we were pretty well hapless. For the ten years we occupied it, the interior of our first home resembled a senior-year college dorm: crappy old furniture, broken miniblinds, and pictures hung randomly over nails that already happened to be sticking out of the walls. Our present home is furnished and decorated as if adults live here, but we haven't been in it long, so give us time. The outlet in one of the boys' bedrooms stopped working last winter. As of this summer, we still haven't gotten around to having it fixed. Insulation hangs exposed over the side of the dishwasher, where the glass tiling I envisioned has yet to materialize. The cat is working on re-texturizing the freshly painted walls, and the boys are beating back the lovely St. Augustine turf, planted fifty years ago by the original owner, one runner at a time, pocketed on her walks through the neighborhood. We help by forgetting to water it. While it would sound noble to chalk our negligence up to our preference for spending time with our kids and each other over salaried jobs, a maid, and lawn service, that wouldn't be the whole truth. It's true that we are perpetually short on money, time, and energy, but it is also true that we simply aren't on the ball.

I've heard that ducks, or maybe geese, only have a set number of offspring, because that number is as high as they can count. I am definitely one over my cognitive limit. Even a freestyle outing, like going to the park, taxes my stunted left brain, since it seems to be against some law of physics for three boys to move in one direction. I go hoarse shouting, "Come back!" "Too far!" "Not in the creek!" "Where's your brother?" I sound like an especially high-strung border collie.

I'm not strong on organization to begin with. I once boiled a pan of eggs dry because I was using the egg timer in another room to help me stay on task and focused. Now imagine what soccer is like for someone like me, faced with the problem of allocating three kids, two parents, and one minivan across overlapping practice times, overlapping game times, and fields that are not even remotely near one another. I need a topographic scale model to work it all out.

Other people probably figure this stuff out in their heads. Other people probably don't program text alerts to their phones reminding them to "pick up kids after school" and "make supper" and "put the kids to bed." I suppose other mothers just notice their children are not home, or are hungry, or have fallen asleep in their clothes on the floor. It blows my mind that there are so many women who are not only responsible for domestic operations, but hold outside jobs that require them to be fully dressed and out the door before nine o'clock each day. I have dropped my kids at school while wearing my pajamas under a trench coat, and I'm already getting up at six in the morning.

I can't imagine having to have my personal grooming act together in addition to serving breakfast, packing lunches, and signing homework.

I was somewhat prepared for the physical and emotional exertion of raising children. I knew there'd be sweat and tears. But I had no idea how mentally challenging the gig would be. Planning and strategy is a huge aspect of it. I am the family secretary, social director, and chief purchaser. I plan menus, oversee nutrition, do the budgeting, pay the bills, maintain the filing, schedule appointments, coordinate recreation, and liaise on my kids' behalf with teachers, room parents, coaches, health professionals, and other parents. That's on top of all the cooking, cleaning, driving, and schlepping.

Needless to say, balls get dropped. At least one school morning every semester, the clean clothes and the groceries run out together, and I have to convince the children that it's all a splendid adventure to wear yesterday's underwear and sprinkle cinnamon sugar on toasted stale heels of bread. But then there are days I can't pull it off, when the tide of domesticity rises up and engulfs me the minute my feet hit the floor. Sometimes so many balls drop, it feels like I am up to my neck in them, adrift in a Ball Pit of Despair.

I would like to be better at managing life. It bothers me when our habitat goes all to hell. I feel bad for our kids. I also grew up with creative, right-brain parents who couldn't seem to get it together domestically, and shame can still flare up over certain household tasks to which I've inherited allergies. Lawn maintenance is one such hot spot. The house I was raised in sat on a large corner lot, shaded by several majestic maple trees, with bluegrass that grew shin-high. There were deep craters that the dog had dug, various small critter graves marked by Popsicle-stick crosses, and a picket fence like a hockey player's teeth, with a few more gaps each year. We had dandelions. Lots and lots of dandelions.

My mother loved them. My sister and I would bring dandelion bouquets to her, and she would coo over them as if they were hothouse orchids. They would go straight into jelly glasses to adorn the table. We made dandelion wreaths for our necks and tucked them in our hair. We made curlicues by peeling strips of the hollow stems backward like string cheese. We used the sticky, bitter milk inside for "glue," artfully adhering leaves together. One spring my parents picked the tender new leaves and cooked them as greens. We made thousands upon thousands of wishes, blown heaven high on dandelion fluff.

My sister and I inhabited our landscape completely and intimately. We explored it, smelled it, tasted it, dug in it, grew in it. I can still call to mind, in microscopic detail, every square foot of that yard. It was our ecosystem, our habitat.

The first inkling I had that there was anything imperfect about our Eden must have been around age eight. I had a friend whose house was always immaculate and whose lawn was always trimmed. One day, I presented her mother with a dandelion bouquet, picked from the strip of earth that ran between the driveway and the house. "Weeds," she said, and tossed them out. I knew then that something about me, my family, and our yard was not right.

There was constant tension between my parents and our neighbors, who did not appreciate dandelions either, or our maple trees, which shaded their grass and littered their yard with leaves and seedlings. I doubt they read my father's books, but if they did,

I wonder what they made of his poem about "The Dandelion Killers," which framed green versus yellow as a clash of values, with ours as the just cause. Dad could spin any act of negligence as a political statement. People who saved money and paid bills on time did so because they were materialistic and greedy. People who voted in elections and served in civic positions were complicit in a corrupt system. People who weeded their lawns were repressed and conforming. I wanted to enjoy the moral high ground, but I secretly worried we were not on the right side of the war.

I grew up, and moved 2,500 miles away to the same house and yard. I was three months pregnant with our first child when we rented the two-bedroom bottom half of an old, rambling foursquare that had been converted to upstairs/downstairs apartments. I gave birth in our bedroom there.

"Is that right? I was born here, too," our landlord said thoughtfully, standing with us on the wide front porch the following spring, having stopped by to fetch something out of the attic. We got a call from the property manager that week. The owner wanted us to have the house. Ours would be the second family to own it in a century. Were we interested? With no savings and scant credit, we were years from being homeowners. Yes, we said anyway. With a small down payment from my widowed father-in-law, and ridiculously kind terms from the seller, it was ours. Or, at least, the mortgage was.

Like my childhood home, our house was on a large corner lot, which meant the portion of yard exposed to public view was double. It is too hot in Arkansas for either the large maples or bluegrass of my northern childhood, but crabgrass thrived and grew high under our laissez-faire regime, and though I know for certain there were none when we moved in, we had dandelions.

A few more every spring. I cooed over every one that was proudly handed to me, strangled in a little fist. When they turned white and star-tipped, the boys blew wishes all over the neighborhood, all over our neighbors' uniformly green lawns. They dug holes and piled rocks and sometimes when I turned into our driveway, I worried that I was still not on the side of the righteous.

Some days I could transcend it and smile at the latest excavation in the front yard, the stick figures drawn in permanent ink on the clapboard siding, new dandelions coming up through the cracks in the sidewalk, all my own wishes sending down roots. At such moments, I felt loving toward the threadbare couch and warped floorboards, not minding that things were shabby and worn if they were comfy and sunlit. Other days I'd wake up thinking we should just sell the place and move. Then I'd realize I would still have to clean it, and weep.

One night I finally got around to replacing the bulbs in the track-lighting fixture above the dining room table, days after the last one had finally gone out. Our oldest son, who was in first grade at the time, and had to do homework on that table, was openly astonished at the difference a little electric light made. "Wow," he said, without even a trace of sarcasm, "I wonder why it took so long to change the lights."

"I don't know," I told him. "I don't know why." I was still standing on the table, and he looked so small and amazed that I wanted to fall to my knees, hold him to my chest and say I'm sorry, I wanted to be better for you. I thought I might have it together by now, but I don't, and I don't think I will before you figure it out and can see for yourself that other people seem to have the secret to life and we, your parents, don't have a clue.

The problem is not with our intelligence. It's with our kind of intelligence. In Myers-Briggs personality type parlance, Patrick and I are both NFPs, which stands not just for neurotic, flaky, and procrastinating, but also for iNtuitive, Feeling, and Perceptive. In practical terms, it means neither of us has a scrap of common sense. Our predominant functions are developed at the expense of sensory perception, linear thinking, and rational decision making. To illustrate: When a lightbulb goes out in the homes of people at the opposite end of the personality spectrum, they (1) notice right away that it is dark; (2) swiftly and correctly deduce the cause of being in the dark; (3) go immediately to the closet where a supply of spare bulbs is kept; (4) change the bulb, properly disposing of the old one; and (5) make a note to replace the spare bulb the next time they are at the hardware store getting lawn supplies. We try not to associate with such people, except that it appears our firstborn is one of them. We are his cross to bear.

With us, a nonemergency malfunction can go unresolved indefinitely. Being in the dark falls under "nonemergency." Other nonemergencies include anything growing or not growing outside; anything a spare bathroom can't compensate for; and strange noises coming from anything with moving parts as long as the parts are still working and not yet on fire, at which point we will most likely notice the problem and make a determination as to whether the object in question is essential and constitutes an emergency. There are very few situations that are automatically labeled urgent. A laundry equipment malfunction is one of them.

A few years ago, we got into a conversation with a childless couple who had just visited the local warehouse club for the first time. They were having a chuckle over the giant containers. "It would take us a *year* to use that much laundry detergent!" they snorted.

"Yeah. We go through one of those a month," I said. In a family of five, two loads a day is the minimum it takes to keep dirty clothes from backing up and overflowing into the hallways. Just changing socks and underwear is a quarter of a load.

One Saturday afternoon our washing machine got through agitating a load of clothes, and then, drunk on power, decided to agitate *me* by refusing to drain. I twiddled the dial and pulled the knob and wiggled the basket, and then I told Patrick the situation.

"Holy shit," he said, before retreating to his office.

I gave him a few minutes, then followed him back there.

"I think it's clogged," I offered.

"Could be," he nodded, avoiding eye contact.

I felt he could use a prompt, so I asked, "What needs to happen for us to find out?"

"Let me think about that."

"Could you think about it *quickly*?" This elicited an injured look. I ignored it. It was no time for kid gloves, and I've poked through all the fingers on mine anyhow. My husband is a man of innumerable charms and gifts, but being quickly roused to action is not one of them. "Let me think about that" is usually a euphemism for "Let me *not* think about that for as long as it can possibly be put off."

It's bad enough we are two NFPs, but he has to go and complicate it by being an introvert. That means his brain has four stomachs. All information has to be chewed twice before he can digest it. I am an extrovert. I think fast and out loud. I process verbally. My opinions develop on the scene, and are revised constantly. I'm like the twenty-four-hour news cycle, complete with screen crawl. Becoming educated about these differences has helped us navigate through many a minefield of potential misunderstanding. He has learned that the words "talk" and "later" uttered in the same sentence will cause me to chew my own leg off. I have learned that the deer-in-the-headlights stare I get in response to "Hey, let's . . ." is not necessarily an out-of-hand rejection. Sometimes, if I stand back and give him a little air, he will come around on his own. Occasionally, I have to bring out the smelling salts.

In this instance, time was not on our side. The laundry clock was ticking. Towels were being used, clothes worn. I needed a specific commitment. I extracted a promise of "first thing in the morning." Morning came, and with it, low groans and complaints of a bad back. Toward lunchtime, I was directed to clear off the top of the appliances and bail out the wash water so he could examine the patient. It was a transparent stalling maneuver, but I prepped as told.

"It's ready for you," I announced, thirty minutes later. He pointed to a sandwich on his desk.

"I have to eat lunch," he said, resolutely, as if the union was behind him. He lifted a potato chip to his mouth, took a bite from it, chewed it one hundred times, put it down, lifted the sandwich to his mouth, took a bite from it, chewed it one hundred times, put it down, and reached for the rest of the first chip. He did all of this in slow motion, like it was his last meal. If I kept watching, it would be, so I returned to the operating theater and pulled the washer out from the wall. I sized up the hose and pipe attachments in back. How hard could this be? I Googled "washing machine clogged drain," and scrolled through a bunch of do-it-yourself forums. Piece of cake. By the time Patrick moseyed into the kitchen for cookies, I was wedged between the wall and washer, trying to loosen a hose connector by hand.

"Are you sure you don't want me to do that?" he offered, peering down over the control panel.

"Not on your life," I grunted. By my reckoning, I was sitting on a gold mine of spousal guilt. Having missed his moment to save the day, Patrick would be driven to overcompensate in other matters of household maintenance. His masculine pride was on the line.

Apparently not. "I find this incredibly sexy, you know," he said, handing me a wrench and leering, as I squatted in the corner with my skirt hitched up and rubber gloves on. My plan was backfiring. "Never learn to type," my feminist mother warned me in junior high. "Or someone will always expect you to." She'd have disowned me for the stunt I pulled next, but I could see that my plunge into D-I-Y was setting a precedent from which there was no return. If I fixed the washer, what stood between me and the lawn mower? Me and the plumbing snake? Me and the engine oil filter? It's not that I believe labor should be divided on the basis of gender—I was raised Free to Be . . . You and Me. But I don't believe doubling my labor on the basis of ability either.

"Here," I said, handing over the wrench. "I can't unscrew the hose. It's too hard for me." Patrick looked skeptical. I batted my eyelashes. Then pouted. "*You* should be doing this anyway."

"Why?" he asked. "Don't you feel proud of yourself tackling this? Doesn't it make you feel capable? Like I feel when you leave me alone to take care of the kids for the day?" He had a point there. But I wasn't about to give it to him. For us, and for every couple I know with young children, division of household labor and parental involvement is an ongoing, perpetually unresolved negotiation, fraught with mistrust and suspicion. It's hard because raising a family is hard work, more work than any two people without a full domestic staff or an endless supply of selfless relatives can accomplish without yelling at each other sometimes. Each party feels he or she is getting screwed somehow, and not in a way that feels good. Throw in sleep deprivation, the elimination of a salary, and responsibility for handling body waste that is not your own, and every day that we don't eat our young is a kind of miracle.

It was my choice to stay at home with our children during the early years, and I wouldn't have traded it for whatever middle-income wage I could have earned at the time. Notwithstanding real financial sacrifice, I was lucky to have the choice, and I knew it. But choosing to be at home didn't waive my right to resent the hell out of it sometimes, especially when Patrick came home from his day at the office with the feeling that he was entitled to relax. His working hours were clearly delineated, whereas I was on call 24/7. On the other hand, it wasn't as if I was tied to a desk all day, every day. I could take my work to the park. My clients were the people I loved most in the world, even if they couldn't wipe their own noses. My colleagues were my best girlfriends. There were no common denominators to form the basis of an objective comparison between our workloads, just vague jealousies that erupted periodically into open recriminations.

"When do I get a weekend off?" I'd mutter, flinging back the sheets to get up on a Sunday morning and make breakfast, while

Patrick snoozed, oblivious to hungry kids clamoring on my side of the bed.

"You got to hang out with your friends today," he'd observe, surveying dirty teacups on the coffee table and post-playgroup wreckage strewn over the floors.

"I wouldn't call it hanging out," I'd say, indignantly. "Would you say you were hanging out with your co-workers all day?" The analogy was a false one, however. I did get to hang out with the friends my children made me, one of the chief benefits of my vocation. But it was hardly leisure time, either. Hosting playgroup was like having a tea party, but one in which two or three chimpanzees accompanied each guest. Going out for any activity was a major operation. I learned to weigh the schlep factor against the merit of being at any given destination. More often than not, that calculation came out to "Nah."

Even a day at the beach is no day at the beach. About once a year, a girlfriend and I take our six kids on a day trip to a lake in the country. It takes half the morning just to pack and coordinate, the rest of the morning to get to our destination. We arrive on the sizzling asphalt parking lot at high noon, a cascade of totes, containers, and inflatables spilling out of our vans. Thirty minutes later, we are all still on the asphalt, inflating, sunscreening, and unloading passengers and equipment. The first time we went, I brought not one, but two magazines for my reading pleasure. Just in case I got all the way through the first and was stuck for something to do. Three exhausting hours later, they went back into the van untouched. Idly thumbing through the glossies is not something you can do in between catering, lifesaving, and commanding a vinyl flotilla. We do have fun. But it isn't hanging out.

It's more like being the roadie for a band. For starters, there's the sheer physical exertion: the endless lifting, hauling, setting up, and tearing down. "Put it over here, no, over there, there, *there*!" Then there is the ass-wiping, the puking, the tantrums, the trashing of rooms. There is the procurement of playmates. And the ridiculous demands about food. The gig sounds more fun than it is. The thing is, though, even on the worst days, it still beats a straight job. There are nights when the lights go down, and I stand in the boys' bedroom doorway with as much awe and gratitude as any starstruck stagehand ever felt standing in the wings.

One such night, I paused to eavesdrop in the hall as Patrick tucked the boys in.

"Do you know what I want to be when I grow up, Daddy?" I heard my firstborn say. I waited, expecting an elaboration on his recent ambition to become the night watchman in a museum.

"What?"

"A Cub Scout den leader." I thought my heart would just give out then and there, because that night it had been my first turn at leading his Cub Scout den.

If "Be Prepared" is the Scout motto, "Wing It" is mine. I still didn't have my leader uniform. I read the meeting literature for the first time that day over lunch. I scribbled a plan on an index card, and ran to the dollar store a couple of hours before the meeting with the only two dollars I had in my pocket to pick up supplies. We made crafts and performed a skit. I not only got through it, I had apparently upheld the dignity of the office sufficiently to trump museum night watchman in the shining eyes of my son. Somehow, I had managed to pull it off.

On a tall shelf against his bedroom wall, I could see the newest race car in his pinewood fleet, complete with tail fins and a chrome paint job, just as he had sketched it for his father. Somehow, Patrick pulled it off, too.

Somehow, I guess we always do.

5.

# Ring of Fire

On our sixth wedding anniversary, the eve of his fortieth birthday, my husband decided to surprise me by cutting off his shoulder-length blond hair.

"Surprise!" he said, as he came through the door, grinning self-consciously and holding up his lopped-off ponytail with the guileless charm of a little boy clutching a fistful of dandelions.

"Surprise," I said weakly, handing him the damp test stick with its pink vertical lines like bars on a tiny prison window. Impossibly, in spite of being on the pill, breast-feeding a toddler, and the almost complete absence of opportunity, I was pregnant with our third child, and his fourth.

Slack-jawed, Patrick stared at the stick. His mouth closed, opened, closed again.

"You're not," he said.

"I am," I said.

He stared back at the stick, and I thought I saw comprehension dawn on his stricken face.

"You *peed* on this," he said finally, looking back to me for confirmation. I wasn't sure whether he was asking if there could be some kind of mix-up, or if he just found it distasteful. I nodded soberly, thinking that the unfolding scene was already completely unsuitable for the baby's memory book. We would have to lie.

Patrick slumped into the nearest chair, still clasping his limp hank of hair. Looking at it, I was reminded of that famous O. Henry short story "The Gift of the Magi," where Della sells her hair to buy her husband, Jim, a chain for his heirloom pocket watch. Only it turns out that Jim has sold the watch for a hair ornament, and both gifts are useless. Of course, it all works out in time for Christmas, and in the end they realize that what matters most is that they have each other. Except in our version, the husband plummets into a spectacular midlife tailspin, during which time the wife is out of her mind with rage, hormones, and confusion, and there are children who need help with wiping whether or not right now is a good time.

There were days I didn't think we would make it to the next week, let alone Christmas. Here's what they don't tell you to expect in *What to Expect When You're Expecting*, or any other pregnancy how-to book I've ever read: Even the most carefully planned and anticipated pregnancy can rock a marriage on a seismic scale. It can test a relationship like few other things can, and show exactly where the fault lines lie. In the space of two blurry years, we had gone from two of us to five of us, with the birth of our first two children and the temporary custody of a third from my husband's previous marriage. We loved each other and our kids, but in the course of keeping up with even the minimum demands of parenting, a few things had gotten pushed to the back burner. Big things, like sleep and sex; and little things, like good books and long kisses.

We weren't relating to each other as lovers, or even as friends— only as stereotypes. Patrick was cast in the part of wayward son. Me, the overbearing mother. It was awful, a cat-and-mouse game that reinforced us as adversaries with every round. He avoided, I nagged. I persecuted, he went underground. His office became his bunker, and his days there encroached into night. After supper, he'd kiss me with a weary sigh, as if being dragged out of the house against his will. I bought it for a while. Advertising agencies are notorious for excessive expectations of overtime. Don't bother coming in Monday if you don't come in Sunday, goes the joke, which everyone in the business knows isn't, really. He's working hard to support us, I'd think. Poor guy. I could ride that glass coach till midnight.

"I thought you were coming home two hours ago," I'd seethe into the phone, when the enchantment wore off.

"What do you want me to do? Miss the deadline? Lose the account?" He always had me there.

"I just want you to come home."

"I'm coming," he'd promise.

But he wouldn't come, and we'd run through the exact same lines a couple of hours later, at a shriller pitch. It was making me crazier and crazier, angrier and angrier. I upped the offensive, demanding to know who else was working late, why it always fell to him to save the day, what, exactly, he was doing there all by himself, night after night. I was determined to get to the bottom of things. I pressed for details, playing both good cop and bad cop, feigning interest and sympathy, then bringing the heat. I accused him of not wanting to come home.

The trouble with getting to the bottom of things, says my mother, who knows, is that there you are, at the bottom.

"You're right," he finally said to me, when I'd called him in a rage, after waking up to find myself still alone at three o'clock in the morning. I'd pried my way through his excuses, one after the other, like I was tearing up rotten floorboards with a crowbar. And then I fell through. Stripped of pretense, his voice was flat and lifeless. "I don't want to come home."

There it was, the bottom.

"Then don't," I said, crying. "Don't come home. Ever."

It sounds maudlin and terrible. It was maudlin and terrible. I could leave it at that and let you think I was the long-suffering wife, and he was the cold-hearted bastard. (Go ahead, think it for a minute, before I get to the next part. He has that much coming.) But it was Kabuki theater, love suicide. Those were painted-on feelings, and we were lost in our roles.

Mothering is a tremendous force. It can possess you completely, eclipsing every other passion, point of view, and relationship. Maybe I was especially vulnerable to being possessed because I had never really consciously identified with my maternal side, and it snuck up on me. Maybe it was because Patrick was used to being bossed around by his mother, and her death during my first pregnancy created a vacuum that sucked me in. Maybe it's just what happens. It's what happened with me, anyway. I had control issues, especially when it came to parenting. It was my way exactly or it was child endangerment. That's literally how I saw it. I was the ultimate, infallible authority where the kids were concerned, benevolent and omnipotent unless crossed. Then, off with his head.

When a parent with control issues is constantly broadcasting the message that the other parent can't be trusted to make decisions or work through problems without advice and direction, they set up a self-fulfilling prophecy. The expectation of failure is loud and clear. There's no chance of acquiring or demonstrating competency when someone is constantly standing over your shoulder, saying, "Not like that. Like this." The parent being critiqued and managed is robbed of the opportunity to figure things out by trial and error, and being a parent is *all* trial and error. There's no other way to learn it except by doing it. You wobble along, and it's in the process of making adjustments that the foundation of your relationship with your child is laid. If anyone besides the baby had told me, "You're doing it wrong," the first time I held, fed, or changed him, it would have destroyed whatever shred of confidence I had as a new mother. I would have been devastated. But I said it to Patrick again and again, if not in those words, with a look and a sigh as I stepped in and took over. I'd elbow him aside and complain that he didn't show more initiative. I'd issue orders and fault him for being passive. I'd critique his interactions with his children, and shame him for not being more engaged. I stripped him of his self-worth and his dignity.

And then I wondered why he wouldn't come home.

He withdrew to his office like a teenager to his room, surrounded by his guitars and comic books. He was drinking too much, sleeping too little, and if I hadn't been so insane myself, I might have seen sooner that the man I knew and loved had checked out some time ago. If I was capable of being honest with myself, I had, too. Each of us crept outside the marriage to steal what the other would not give. He wanted space. I wanted a devoted husband and father. The one I found was already someone else's, but it didn't matter to me. We were just friends, spending time together. Granted, it was lot of time, and if you counted the time I was spending with him in my head, it was most of the time. I wasn't in love, but I loved to be with this man. He was gallant and swaggering, a take-charge kind of guy. He bristled protectively when I alluded to my lonely nights, and if I didn't actually lean my head on his shoulder, I let myself picture it there.

He was a family man, and that quality that made him so attractive to me would have probably kept us both out of real trouble, regardless, but my surprise pregnancy was a timely intervention. Even so, I was slow to shift my emotional focus back to my marriage. It had drifted further than I was prepared to admit. One night, I woke up from a vivid dream where I was standing opposite my friend, our palms on each other's hearts. It was an intimate gesture Patrick and I had picked up along the way, a way of connecting. The image was jolting, much more than had it been sexually explicit. I took it as a wake-up call, calling me back from the brink before any harm was done.

But harm was done. What a person doesn't know can hurt them. To someone looking at my marriage from the outside in, it would have looked very much like one or both of us was having an affair. Neither of us was screwing around. But neither were we being faithful to each other. It looked nearly the same as if someone was cheating, and it felt nearly the same. Only there was no one outside of the marriage who we could point to and say, he or she is partly to blame. It was all on us.

We still loved each other, but we were not at the top of our game. Facing another round of pregnancy and infancy was more than we could do gracefully. And so we were blundering our way through it, pelting each other with resentment and blame. In and of themselves, our grievances were unexceptional. They all came down to how we divided available time and energy. In fatter years, we could have arbitrated with more civility. But this was famine, and we were starving people fighting over the last thin scrap.

Every emotion and perception was amplified and distorted. "You always" and "You never" became the constant, looping refrain. It felt like our wedding bands had twisted into Möbius strips—around and around we'd go, never getting to the other side.

I have a friend who has managed to maintain a vital and dynamic relationship with her husband for more than thirty years. She says the secret is very simple: they just have to be willing to renegotiate everything, forever. It was time for Patrick and me to sit down at the bargaining table. We both had unmet needs, wants, and demands. This was a serious test of our marriage. It deserved and required our undivided energy and attention. We needed to be in lockdown at Camp David, with a full entourage of aides and interpreters. We needed bottled spring water and frequent stretch breaks; guided meditations and long, quiet walks in the woods. We needed all calls held and nothing on each day's agenda but working out a new deal.

But we had kids. There were clothes to wash, baths to run, library books to return, and crusts to cut. We couldn't scream, or cry, or curse, as loud or as long as we sometimes needed to. And yet, as much as the presence of children inhibited and hindered us, I am not sure we would have hung in there without them. In a way, they were our entourage: a steadying influence that kept us from walking away on days when it felt too fucking hard.

The urge to escape was strong. On our worst days, I thought I might as well have an affair. I fantasized about leaving, or making him leave. Then I'd remember I was three months pregnant and he was my sons' father, and there was the house, the money, and all this *stuff* we shared. As hard as it was to stay in my marriage, it seemed a whole lot harder to get out of it. That, right there, is the whole point of marriage as an institution. There's legal and financial infrastructure that can't be dismantled overnight, no matter how badly you want to walk away. And if children are part of what you've built up together, you can't tear the whole thing down anyway, because you tear them up with it. You can only rearrange the particulars: who and what goes where, and with whom.

There were days that the only thing holding me back from kicking him out was the thought that my pain-in-the-ass husband would be an even bigger pain-in-the-ass ex-husband. And I would have to put up with him, because of the children. As long as I was stuck with him anyhow, I might as well keep him close enough to take out the trash and help with bedtime.

I find the flip side of this line of reasoning useful even today.

"I will be the ex-wife from hell," I promise sweetly, whenever I catch him admiring someone younger, blonder, and bouncier in the side-view mirror. He chuckles and gives a heartfelt "whoo-whee." Today, I like to think, he is happy to be stuck with me.

Nobody should have to stay in a relationship that's broken beyond repair, but there's something to be said for sealing off the exits. Being legally trapped together should be the right of any committed couple willing to endure it. When you've got to turn and face each other, there's a chance you can work it out.

Patrick did come home that night, and I let him stay, because we didn't know what else to do. After three nights sleeping apart and two days not speaking, we went to a marriage counselor. Her name was Nancy. She hardly said much of anything. She didn't have to. Just having a neutral third party in the room made us more mindful and aware of what we were saying to each other and how we said it. It didn't take long to turn things around. Our issues weren't the insurmountable, irreversible barriers they had felt like. We weren't the bad people we felt like. The issues were just issues, and we were just people who needed to upgrade a few skills. The fact that we both kept showing up for our weekly sessions became visible evidence of our commitment to each other, and that goodwill began to spread into the other days of the week. A kind word here, a soft gesture there. We were still so fragile in that first month or so of therapy. If we came up against any degree of conflict, we would back away from each other as if from a fallen wire. "Let's save this for Nancy," we'd agree, and somehow manage to avoid it until then. By the time we got to Nancy, the issue in question wouldn't seem like such a big, snaky thing anymore. Gingerly, we began to try it at home. Clutching our photocopied diagrams of "How to Practice Active Listening," we'd approach a topic like students learning a foreign language. "I think, uh, no, wait . . . I feel . . . you should, no, wait. What was the question?"

The birth of our third and last child mirrored love's labor. My prior two birthing experiences had started out as all-natural, at-home deliveries. The first was successful, but there were complications with the afterbirth that required a night in the hospital;

the next labor was long and painful, and ended with an emergency C-section. I was younger, and cockier then, and very controlling. When things didn't go according to plan, I had a hard time accepting it, and added unnecessarily to my fear and pain. The third time was different. I still had ideals, but I was willing to let go of expectations. I didn't have anything to prove, but only wanted what was best for me and my baby. I hoped to avoid another caesarean, but neither did I want to repeat a long and difficult labor before winding up in the operating room anyway. I had to trust my doctor, accept advice, and be ready to make compromises. I gave myself permission to ask for help, and seek relief, if I needed it. I had a birth plan that I took seriously, but held lightly.

When our son was born, the sun was setting outside the delivery room. I felt no pain. I had no fear. Patrick stood at my side, holding my hand, his golden hair haloed by the dying sky. Our eyes burned into each other, as if we were the only two people in the room, in this marriage. But we weren't. This birth would add to all that was already between and behind us, binding us and holding us, sometimes against our will.

He squeezed my hand, hard, and with everything I had, I bore down and pushed.

# 6

# Penis Ennui

A friend of mine changed her daughter's diaper in front of me the other day. I couldn't hide my shock, and let out a little gasp.

"What?" my friend said.

"No penis," I said, pointing.

Of course, I knew there wouldn't be. It wasn't like she'd cross-dressed the baby and I'd been duped. I have plenty of friends with daughters. I've seen vulvas. It happens that I own one. But having changed my own children's bottoms approximately 18,000 times, I am conditioned to expect a penis inside a diaper. When there isn't one, I experience an irrational jolt of panic, as if maybe it fell off.

In our family, penises are standard-issue equipment. We have four of them, or rather, they do, my husband and our three sons.

I am the odd woman out, the minority. It's not how I was raised. I had a sister, a mother, and a father. No brothers. Females were the ruling class, and I was part of it. I don't remember ever plunging ass-first into a toilet bowl in the house where I grew up. Not much was constant or predictable about life at 20 Armstrong, but you could reliably count on the seat to be down, day or night. It was there for me.

In my adult home, vertical is the default position for the toilet seat. Patrick and the boys seem to view it as a kind of Murphy bed. Available if needed, but otherwise up and out of their way. If there were toilet seats with spring-loaded hinges that snapped down like mouse traps, I would install them. Instead, I give shrill demonstrations in seat raising and lowering, which have a deterrent effect, but not in the way intended. The boys become reluctant to raise the seat in the first place, and pee all over it. Every time I have to wipe the fixtures behind them, which is every time they go, I wonder why we don't just rip all the moving parts out. The technology—seat hinges and flush lever— is evidently too complicated for them.

I've heard that some European public toilets are simply self-flushing stainless-steel closets. I wish IKEA would figure out how to flat-pack one. They could call it the PIPÜ. The boys could have that, and I would have my very own bathroom, a sanctuary of glistening ceramic, with a deadbolt on the door and a toilet seat cemented to the rim. I could even put a rug on the floor, right next to the pedestal, which in reality has to be wiped down at least once a day with window cleaner.

"I just wiped here this morning!" I yell. "Seriously, how hard can it be to control a penis?"

Patrick shrugs. "Pretty hard, sometimes." There's no point in getting technical. The kinesiology and pneumatics, if he could explain them, would be lost on me, a stranger in a strange land. No matter how long I live among penises, I'll never really understand them. I'm like a mechanic who services imported cars but has never actually been behind the wheel of one. I don't know how they handle, first thing in the morning, bursting to pee. Apparently, like a fire hose.

The boys love to hear the story about the time I was changing one of their diapers on our bed, in the dark, when Patrick woke up shouting and flailing. I froze where I stood, a clean diaper dangling from my suspended hand. Was he having a nightmare? A heart attack? After a few seconds of incoherent cursing, he became conscious enough to realize, and convey, the source of his distress.

"The baby! The diaper! Cover the baby!"

"Huh?"

I looked down to where I had positioned the baby horizontally on the bed. I could just make out the last droplets of a stream that had arced impressively over his own head and splashed down on his father's. I flung the clean diaper over the source, but it was too late. I threw another over Patrick's face, trying to be helpful.

"Always," he sputtered, "cover that thing during changes."

Well, how was I to know it would go off like that?

Ten years later, my son still regales his younger brothers with "the time I peed on Dad's head." They hoot and slap the ground. Way to get one over on the alpha male. More, and worse, potty talk inevitably follows, accompanied by pantomime where indicated. Somebody farts. Then everybody farts. More hooting. More farting. I pretend I am Jane Goodall, living among the chimps. It seems less beneath me that way.

*Today, the smallest male was observed urinating off the front porch,* I mentally narrate from behind a blind of laundry. *At feeding time, one of the troupe passed gas loudly, which caused much excitement among the other juveniles.*

"Wait!" someone shouts. "I've got to go pee!" There is the pounding of sneakers through the hall, the crash of the doorknob as it hits the inside bathroom wall, a forceful hiss that fades to a tinkle, footsteps receding, the screen door slamming shut.

*I am conducting an experiment to see if the subjects can be taught to raise and lower a simple hinged mechanism,* I tell myself as I open the bathroom closet, reach for the window spray and paper towels, and turn to face the toilet.

*So far, it is unsuccessful.*

"I have a son," I said, for the first time to anyone.

Through the telephone, there came a soft, trembling sigh, a breath of pure tenderness. "Oh," said my father, calling me by my baby name, *"Kiki."*

Moments before, giving birth in my own bedroom, I had never felt more a grown woman. "Kiki," he said, and I was four years old. *Look what I made, Daddy. It's a surprise.*

It's a boy.

"A *boy?*" my mother said. She was as shocked as I was. Babies in our family were girls. What other kind was there? "We like to keep it a mystery," I told the ultrasound technician when I declined to learn the baby's gender. But there was no mystery. I'd always known I would have a girl. We referred to our child as "she," exclusively, right up to the moment I saw her penis.

I couldn't believe it. "A boy!" I said, laughing. "Oh my God, a boy!"

I have a son.

Saying those words made me feel mighty and mythic, like an empress or a pioneer. I embraced them. I was head over heels in love with my new man. I could wait a little longer for a girl.

I was pregnant again the following year, and my dreams of a daughter were reawakened. I monitored my body for any variation from my first pregnancy. Differences in weight gain, nausea, appetite, heartburn, muscle aches, cravings, or aversions were all evidence that I was gestating a girl. I researched sex determination to learn if there were factors of conjugal timing or position that might have tipped the chances in an X chromosome's favor. What I learned was that it was wholly up to the sperm to deliver the goods. Human eggs come only in grade XX. It's an X or Y sperm that gets the deciding vote on gender, and the odds are inherited through the father's line. It was all on Patrick.

I added up the chromosomes. Patrick had only a brother, and between them, they had sired only sons. I scrambled a branch higher up the family tree. His father had only a brother. I went to visit my father-in-law, intent on shaking out an aunt or two. As he walked me through ancestral gravestones, touched that I was taking such a keen interest in his roots, my hopes withered. It appeared that my husband's family had lost the recipe for girls somewhere on the wagon trail. His paternal line had produced a grand total of one girl in the last century, a statistic so anomalous that her birth was either a miracle or the fruit of adultery. In either case, Patrick was not directly descended from her, so our odds were not improved.

I had to know. "What is it?" I asked the ultrasound technician, peering at a blob on a screen. It was like sexing an earthworm. I couldn't tell which end was which, let alone identify the parts in between. The technician pointed to a tiny peninsula, dangling in the amniotic sea. "Definitely a boy. No question."

If there was a spark of a chance that the technician didn't know a foot from a penis, I didn't permit myself to kindle it. The baby was healthy, and very much wanted. That's what mattered. His brother would have a buddy. And I wouldn't have to buy new clothes. Not one sweet, pink, smocked, eyeleted scrap. I was keeping a running list of girls' names on a piece of notebook paper, carried over from my first pregnancy. I tucked it away with my memorabilia as a keepsake for the boys, a roll call of their ghost sisters. Good-bye, Sophia Faye. Good-bye, Ruby Evangeline. Good-bye, Genevieve Leigh. I guess I thought I would give birth to a line of Royal Doulton china figurines. Royal Doulton can have the names. Given my sons' DNA, it's highly unlikely that our family will ever have need.

If a trace of wistfulness lingered, it evaporated completely when my second son was born. He was a big baby, nine pounds and change. I felt virile, in mind, if not in clobbered body. I was a mother of men.

My one indulgence in what might have been was an insistence that the baby would be christened in a cathedral-length heirloom gown of Irish linen and lace. Patrick, though long outside the fold, grew up Southern Baptist, a denomination that takes a dim view of infant baptism and cross-dressing. He was nervous about the whole thing.

"This is the only chance I will ever have to see a child of mine in a white gown at the altar," I said. "Deal with it."

It was clear to me that a daughter wasn't in the cards after all, and I was at peace with it. It amplified my growing sense that two children were enough. It had seemed all along like we would have three, but it had also seemed all along like they would be girls, so I wrote it off as fantasy. When I came up pregnant the third time, on the minipill and still breast-feeding, we couldn't help but harbor faint, pink-tinged hope that anything was possible. Very faint. I chose not to learn the baby's sex in advance just so I could pretend he was a girl, until presented with irrefutable evidence to the contrary.

We greeted that evidence in good humor. "I guess this is what I get for being boy crazy all my life," I quipped to visitors. My obstetrician assured me we'd have to go through another two or three boys to get to a girl, based on his own clinical observations and a waggish bedside manner. We asked for a referral to a good urologist. Whether he was right or wrong about the long odds, our family was complete.

It is as it should be. I am the household goddess and queen bee. A girl would present a challenge to my monopoly, as well as my acquired skill set. Little girls are now as strange to me as little boys once seemed. Whenever I babysit one of my friends' daughters, I am at an absolute loss. I'm used to boys coming over and running off with the herd. The girls stay at my elbow, looking up at me expectantly. They want to talk. I never know what to say. "Crayons?" I offer, as if holding out a pack of cigarettes. "Something to read?" It's awkward, like having a foreign exchange student over for tea. Boys are the devil I know.

A very deep dive into the toy box might bring up a disheveled Barbie or remnant pieces of a fiesta-colored tea set to amuse the young mam'zelle, artifacts of my sons' preschool years, when I bought toys according to affirmative action practices, maintaining a careful balance of yin and yang. The inventory was composed mainly of purposeful, primary-colored toys that were gender neutral, European brands that sounded like something you'd find on a cheese board. *Brio en croûte*. There were, in the beginning, a very few pieces of Chinese-manufactured injection-molded plastic, in the way that the farmers of Australia, in the beginning, had very few rabbits. And there were an even number of so-called boys' and so-called girls' toys. There was a yellow enameled metal dump truck. There was a tool set. There were dishes. And a baby doll. "Alan Alda made me do it," I told Patrick, when I brought it home, swaddled in pink. It was a brown baby doll, for added multicultural value. My husband, six years older, and raised in the American South, did not grow up listening to *Free to Be . . . You and Me*, the feminist-themed all-star children's album from the seventies. I belted out the chorus of the duet Alda sang with Marlo Thomas. "William wants a doll, 'cause someday he is gonna be a father, too . . ."

Patrick left the room. "It's all right to cry," I sang after him, breaking into another number.

My son was tender and responsive toward his baby, but only when nudged. He was much more interested in the pleather-corseted fashion doll we called "bondage Barbie," a German knockoff I'd come across before he was born, and acquired as a bit of kinky kitsch. He literally drooled over her, preferring her firm but rubbery legs to any other teether. It was "William Wants a Doll," as reimagined by Camille Paglia. *Free to Be . . . You and Me* meets third-wave feminism.

My middle son showed no interest whatsoever in the baby doll. The youngest seemed to regard it as a competitor in an increasingly strained ecosystem, and kept dropping it on its head.

I finally gave it away, along with the chewed-up Barbie clone. Determined to preserve some measure of equal opportunity for toys in our home through all developmental stages, I bought a yellow Easy-Bake Oven at a garage sale, knowing my four-year-old would love baking up child-size cakes and cookies. I was right. He was beside himself with anticipation of on-demand dessert. We raced off to the toy superstore to find utensils and mixes, which were shelved among the child-size carpet sweepers and plastic fruits. A plastic playhouse was on display in the center aisle, with red shutters and bright yellow flower decals.

"Hey," I said to my son, "that looks pretty neat."

He drew himself up haughtily, clutching his cookie set in its hot pink packaging. "That's a *girl's* toy," he sniffed icily. "I don't play with *girls'* things."

If I couldn't prevent my kids from developing gender biases in the first place, at least I was confusing them. That was something, considering how little ambiguity there is in children's marketing today. Walking into a toy store, you'd never know, unless you remembered that for a brief, shining moment in the late seventies and early eighties, it was sexist to suggest a toy was just for girls, much less label it so. Christmas catalogs in those days showed little boys puttering in plastic kitchens, and little girls hammering nails in birdhouses. A generation later, the advertising and packaging of "girls' toys" has never been more explicit, and froufrou is enjoying a renaissance that makes the baroque era seem austere. I don't think it's men who are to blame for this incarnation of girly-girl, though. I suspect it's driven by moms of my generation who didn't get their fill of boas and rhinestones as children. That's where rationing gets you.

If that's the case, I have probably ensured that my sons will be card-carrying members of the NRA (if not private militias) by drawing the line at the most traditional pastime of American boys: gunplay. For years, not even water pistols were allowed under my watch. Toy swords and plastic light sabers are okay, though a light saber can deliver a pretty good bonk to the head, and I was a bit disturbed when the boys used scissors to trim the foam blades of their swords to a point that could take an eye out. But swords are artifacts, and light sabers are fantasy. I don't lose sleep wondering which of the neighbor kids' dads might be Jedi weapon enthusiasts or weekend pirates. In another country, in another time, I might also view plastic pistols and M-16s as unobjectionable props for a child's warrior play. But we live in the southern United States, and there are real guns all around us, in the cabinets, closets, and garages of our quiet suburban neighborhood, and not just the hunting kind. We live in a state where it is necessary to post signs reminding people not to bring guns with them into schools and libraries. Where a child brandishing a toy pistol was shot dead by police a few years ago. Where accidental deaths of children by guns are common, and where children have opened fire on other children with automatic assault weapons. For me, that takes all the fun out of "Bang, you're dead."

In the beginning, I naively thought I could keep my kids in a bulletproof bubble. Not only were guns banned from our home; the word itself was taboo. A gun was That-Which-Cannot-Be-Named. One day, when my oldest son was two, he built an L-shape with some LEGOs and aimed it at me. I squinted at him.

"What's that?"

"It's a pffffer," he said, knowing what it was, but not what to call it.

I promptly confiscated it.

"No pffffing," I said, firmly.

As he started preschool, and began to make friends whose parents I didn't know well, it became apparent that a strategy of denial was about as realistic and effective an approach to gun safety as abstinence education is to birth control. Parents who don't want their children to have sex or smoke cigarettes or use drugs and alcohol need to talk to their kids about sex, cigarettes, drugs, and alcohol. I needed to talk to mine about guns. Early, and often. Opening up that dialogue had the effect of easing up domestic weapons sanctions—ever so slightly—over time. Sci-fi-style ray guns, when given as gifts, have occasionally been allowed, though they have a way of quietly disappearing after a while. Permission has been granted to carry water guns, too, once a squeeze toy would no longer cut it. "They're water *squirters*," I insist, as we walk out of the dollar store with neon pistols. The older boys even get to shoot BB guns on the Cub Scout practice range. They've been drilled through and through on safety issues, and I can only hope they'll develop an appreciation for the moral ones. I don't try to prevent my kids from playing with their friends' toy machine guns when they are visiting in someone else's home, but I am very comfortable explaining that it's not something we do in ours. My children are the gunplay equivalent of social smokers.

The impulse to arms is something I naively thought I could squelch altogether, but even in my mild-mannered crew, the force proved strong. I've never bought into "Boys will be boys" as an excuse for aggressive behavior. It's a bullshit excuse for anything but armpit farts in my opinion. But a few years on the playground convinced me that boys have an innate drive to express physical valor, to a degree not shared by most girls. I saw it in boys who were taught to be tender, and I saw it in boys who were taught to be tough. To pretend it wasn't there was to deny something essential about my sons' nature.

Before, I had been adamant that differences in how boys and girls played were one hundred percent manufactured. I knew the cultural conditioning was too broad and too deep to completely immunize my children to stereotypes, but I believed that with enough diligence I could give them a healthy resistance. Patrick, a self-described beta male, was mostly an ally in the cause. He didn't tease about the dolls and tea sets, he didn't tell the boys not to cry, and he was unrestrained in physical and verbal expressions of affection. If he raised an eyebrow over a baby doll or a sparkly pony, it was raised discreetly and wryly.

My husband is like most guys of our generation: nurturing, sensitive, open with his emotions, and having to improvise modern fatherhood without any kind of useful precedent. Once, when I was pushing him to spend more hands-on time with the kids, Patrick threw up his hands in honest frustration, and said, "But I'm already a hundred times more involved than my father was with me."

"I know you are," I said, with real sympathy. "And it's still not enough."

We were both exaggerating to make our points. But the core feeling of his statement was true, and I think is true, for most fathers today: They are already doing so much more, and it *still* doesn't feel like enough. It doesn't help that nowhere in popular culture is there an up-to-date map to get us through this new landscape. It's like trying to navigate the interstate system with a road atlas from 1956. With your kids fighting in the backseat and the wife saying, "Well, just *ask* someone."

But who are they supposed to ask? The bumbling idiot dads on television? The evangelical men's groups who want to play *Father Knows Best*? The New Age drumming circles that seem just as nostalgic and contrived? Those don't lead the way forward. And as much as I would like men to take it from Oprah, mommy blogs, women's magazines, and me that *mother* knows best what kind of husbands and fathers they should be, it's not really for us to say. Women can only speak to what it is we think we need from men, and honestly, I'm not too clear on what that is half the time. Be sensitive, but not a sissy. Be strong, but don't cross me. Be totally available to your family, but don't let your career suffer. Be unconditionally supportive, but show some backbone once in a while. Get in touch with your feminine side, man up, and leave the goddamn toilet seat down. Is that really so hard?

I think maybe it is.

I was lucky to be a little girl in North America in the seventies. I felt lucky. Women like Marlo Thomas and Gloria Steinem, and my mother, saw to that. If I ever encountered discrimination based on my gender, it never penetrated the circle the feminist movement drew around me with stories, songs, and mantras that affirmed my equality, and maybe, inadvertently, inevitably, took it a step further. I knew I could be anything I wanted to be when I grew up: a scientist, a writer, a dancer, a mother. A mother of girls, of course. Because girls were celebrated, not boys. Girls, as I understood it, were better. As a kid, I didn't understand that the message I was getting was one of correction. I never got the earlier memo.

I bought the CD version of *Free to Be . . . You and Me* for my boys before they could talk. I was eager to have Marlo and company back me up on dolls for boys, and the righteousness of a good cry. I still love it as memorabilia. But my sons don't seem to connect with it. I don't think it speaks to them. They know it's all right to cry. They know mommies and daddies can be almost anything they want to be (except, respectively, daddies and mommies, according to one song, which did not anticipate the coming of the pregnant man—do I hear a *Free to Be . . . He or She* follow-up?). The subtext of the album is that gender is all in the eye of the beholder, that there is nothing inherently special about being either a girl or a boy.

Years before I had my own kids, I took a walk through the woods with a friend and his son. The boy could not stop picking up rocks along the path and throwing them. I was annoyed. It was a beautiful day. The setting was serene. Why couldn't the child just appreciate the natural surroundings? Why did he have to disturb it? What was the fascination with rocks, anyway? We were nowhere near anything that could break, but in my mind, the rock-throwing was an act of mindless vandalism, typical of the masculine impulse to possess and alter the environment. Just another form of territorial pissing, I crossly thought.

At this moment, or at any other given hour of any given day, one of my sons' hands is likely wrapped around a rock. I find rocks in their pockets, in their backpacks, and in their beds. There are caches of them hidden all over our house and yard. My oldest son, who also happens to be the gentlest, is the most obsessive about them. A naturalist in the Victorian manner, he hoards rocks the way dragons hoard gold. I've been at the losing end of many an emotional standoff when I've tried to keep him from bringing a new specimen home. "What's so special about this one?" I say, exasperated, as he weeps over an ordinary-looking chunk of sandstone. To me it looks the same as the twenty or thirty at home just like it, but he knows each one individually. Something in his steady nature relates to geology. He and the rocks share a language I can't understand, a language of sequence and persistence, the syntax of time.

His brothers may not share the intensity of his obsession, but rocks are a principal preoccupation of theirs, too. They pile them up, move them around, and break them down. Where there is adequate space and supply, they throw them. And when they do, I see it for the joyous act it is, a release of energy that's been bound up in sediment and minerals for millions of years. "Yippee!" I imagine the rock singing, as it finally gets to fly.

Living with boys has changed the way I see men. I used to love them in spite of themselves. I've come to love them because of themselves. Collectively, they can be assholes. But so can women, given the same chance. Anyone who thinks estrogen is the antidote for brutality has neither paid much attention to history nor taken an eighth-grade girls' gym class. Men may have sins against female kind to atone for, but being born male is not one of them.

If acceptance of my destiny came in a single moment, it came one day as the children were gleefully catapulting off the sofa. I was trying to do something in the other room that would best be accomplished unaccompanied by the sounds of squeaky springs and crashing bodies. I stormed in.

"I have HAD it with jumping off the furniture!" I shouted. "From now on, there will be NO MORE JUMPING OFF THE FURNITURE." As I stood there raving, reason left my body and observed me with calm bemusement from the side. *Are you crazy?* it asked. *You have three boys. There will* always *be jumping off the furniture.*

Always, until they grow up and move out, and I am sent back

to civilization, unable to remember anymore if the toilet seat belongs up or down, lonely for the sound of stampeding sneakers and armpit farts, a strange old woman who gestures for you to sit on her sagging couch, presses a rock into your palm, and says, Now. Let me tell you about my years among boys.

# 7

# Back in the Saddle

About three months after our third child was born, my husband and I had sex. We had sex, not out of an explosion of pent-up desire, or a gradual rekindling of attraction, or even out of generic horniness, but because it was going on three months, and it was getting a little embarrassing.

In a rare confluence of events, the children were all asleep early and in their own beds, there was nothing on television, and there was no good reason to not have sex. In short, we did it because we had to. The preliminaries went something like this:

"You wanna?"

"I guess."

A few minutes later we were lying in bed on our backs, covers drawn up to our chins like two shy virgins about to consummate an arranged marriage. We knew what we were supposed to be doing—we just had no idea how to get started. More verbal foreplay:

"Do we have condoms?"

"In the sock drawer? Wait, did you run the dishwasher?"

Oh baby.

We actually own a book of scripted lovemaking, called *101 Nights of Great Sex*, to help with the failures of erotic imagination that kick in somewhere around the thousandth diaper-change mark. The book has tear-out pages with detailed instructions for getting it on more creatively. I bought it after our second son turned a year old. We thought the baby years were mostly behind us and that it might be safe to get back in the water. We have been frugal with it, like survivors on a lifeboat with the last tin of rations. By my reckoning, ninety-five nights of great sex are still up for grabs. At this rate, I figure we can look forward to one or two a year well into our retirement.

In the meantime, there we were, having to improvise. My husband, having decided that someone should *do* something, lunged toward second base. "Not the breasts!" I hissed, blocking him with my elbows. Any contact with them would set the baby off like a car alarm. Breast-fed babies have a biometric feature that enables them to detect mammary trespass through walls. Their heads will detonate by remote if anyone else so much as breathes near their mother's nipples. All infants are exquisitely sensitive to ambient sexual activity, or for that matter, sexual thoughts. A three-month-old will reliably sleep for several hours at a stretch with one parent staring vacantly into a computer and the other watching infomercials in a neighboring room. But a mere

neck-nuzzle on the way to refill the chip bowl releases sex phero-
mones that travel through the baby monitor, into the nursery,
where they scald the baby, who wakes up enraged like the giant
in "Jack and the Beanstalk."

My husband, deflected, but committed now, changed tactics
and dove headfirst under the covers. I thought at first he'd lost a
sock or something.

When I realized what he was up to, it was shocking and kind
of sordid, as in, you want to do *what?* It doesn't seem possible
to forget about something like oral sex, but a few weeks before
that I forgot to pick up my kindergartner from school, so chalk
another one up to chronic sleep deprivation.

Sex after children is like live theater. The longer you go without it, the less you miss it. It strikes you as a silly thing for people
to do. Stacked next to an early bedtime with a good book or TV,
there's no contest. But when you finally go, by the end of the first
act, you're thinking, *Why don't we have season tickets?* I was the
rube in the front row, exclaiming, "Gee, this is *great!*" I thought
about calling some friends, in case they had misplaced their cli-
torises, too.

"It was under the duvet cover all this time!"

It was a bit like finding a needle in the haystack. With three
children under six, personal grooming concerns got reprioritized.
What was maintained depended solely on who was likely to see
it anytime soon. Teeth? School principal, playgroup moms, bug
man. Brush them. Bikini area? Not unless I had a gynecological
exam that week.

I was still hugely pregnant when my toddler got in the tub
with me one evening, and backed up against something fuzzy. He
turned around, saucer-eyed, pointing a quivering finger.

"What's *that?*"

I brought my thighs together as best as I could, and adopted a reassuring tone, as if narrating a wildlife documentary for children's television. "It's Mommy's vagina," I explained.

There was an aghast pause, as he considered how to deal with this . . . unpleasantness. He decided to be blunt.

"I think you need to get out of the bathtub," he suggested with thin civility. Madam, I said *good day.*

Three months postpartum, my vagina was less out there, but I was still self-conscious about it. I couldn't help but worry it was unsettling for my husband, who has, after all, seen heads come out of it. In between pregnancies, it was trim, tame, and kittenish. Then it swelled up and exploded—a gooey purplish creature emerging with a howl, like in a sci-fi movie. I'm sure in the back of his mind Patrick wondered if it was really safe to approach.

Back in the saddle, the ride was beginning to feel a little less bumpy. I was on the verge of really forgetting myself, when my husband, also forgetting himself, went back for the breasts. It must be said that the baby and I were together on the breast-fondling prohibition. Once an erogenous zone, they had become the no-fly zone. There were times I felt like punching Patrick for just looking at them. The cruel irony for him was that they never looked better. I was an A-cup when we met, and he was perfectly fine with that, especially since bras are optional in Canada, and I never wore one. But he must have felt a little cheated when I jumped to a 36D for the babies, like I'd been hoarding the really good ones all that time.

I was like Growing Up Skipper, Barbie's teenybopper cousin in the seventies, whose chest expanded when you cranked her arm. Overnight, I had porn-star boobs. I might have taken some pleasure in the novelty and spectacle, but it was counterweighted by the droopiness of everything else. There is something a little kinky about the nursing bra, like crotchless panties for your chest. But the leaking and spraying milk, the sodden cotton pads bunched up in the bra cups, and the dairy farm rhythm of the electric breast pump soon banished all non-nutritional associations. Controversy over nursing in public was baffling to me. Unbuttoning a blouse had all the eroticism of whipping out a sippy cup. The idea of incorporating my breasts into the act of sex was as much a turnoff as if Patrick suggested bringing some diapers into play. They were ogled, groped, and suckled enough as it was. In between feedings, they were on lockdown.

I intercepted my lover's wandering hands, thinking I could slide them elsewhere without his noticing. But where? Not onto the sad and wrinkled balloon that was my stomach. It has housed three children, and none of them were fashionably compact baby bumps. Just reading the pee-stick with the last one caused my abdominal muscles to bulge out. At full term, I measured four feet around the middle. I am only five feet, four inches tall, and I looked like a beanbag chair. Take the beans out, and you've got a big empty bag. Supine, it lay more or less flat, but that meant sticking to the missionary position, and staying very still. The intersection between looking good and feeling good in the act was increasingly elusive. In a marriage workshop we attended at church, open-eyed lovemaking was recommended as an aid to deeper intimacy. A lovely older couple pointed out that it was important to balance the openness of the eyes with the dimness of the lighting. But that only helps with the visual aspect. The tactile truth is harder to disguise. The breasts were off-limits, and everything else was too squishy, so I continued to hold both my husband's hands tightly in what I hoped would seem like an act of passion.

Before we had kids there would have been no acting about it. Patrick and I were physically combustible from the first moment we got within a hundred feet of each other. We made love indoors and out, in closets, in cars, on the floor, against walls. Once in an underground World War II bunker while tourists wandered overhead. When passion wasn't at a rolling boil, it was on constant simmer. Having three children in five years had the effect of putting the pot into deep freeze for weeks at a time, then trying to thaw and reheat it before anyone woke up and wandered into the kitchen looking for a drink of water. There was hardly time to break the ice, let alone get steamy. We needed more than a moment's notice.

When you are young, childless, and endlessly hot for each other, scheduled sex sounds like a fate worse than celibacy. You vow to drive off a cliff together before it comes to that. Like the man sang, "Better to burn out than fade away." Then you are there, peering down into the chasm of no sex at all, and spontaneity seems like a picky thing to get hung up on, really. It's not like you've got anything *better* to do on Saturday nights. I prefer to call it "premeditated," rather than "planned" because then it sounds less like an appointment, and more like a rendezvous. In theory, you could spin the whole concept as an elaborate fantasy, but if we had time or energy for role-playing, we wouldn't need to premeditate. I'll shoot it to you straight: There's nothing very arousing about a proposition that can be answered with, "Saturday works." But it helps get your head in the game.

In essence, a date for sex with your spouse is not all that different from unmarried dating, except you've both already agreed at the outset how the night will end. It's the children who supply the missing element of suspense. In some contexts, the threat of interruptus lends an erotic urgency to coitus. Back in the day, we enjoyed our share of breathless moments in semiprivate settings. The heart-pounding suspension of sound and motion while you listened for footsteps was a way of prolonging the sweet agony. When the footsteps are little, it's just agony. Nothing kills the mood like an abrupt reminder that the person you are urging your partner to defile harder is somebody's mommy.

The difficulty in getting your freak back on as a mom is as much about finding the headspace as it is scraping together the time, privacy, and energy to do the deed. At the instinctual level, motherhood is essentially conservative in nature. Mother's prime directive is safety and stability, and she for sure does not want a noisy slut in your bedroom while the kids are sleeping down the hall. Accessing the parts of myself that involve risk and self-seeking—my sexuality, my creativity, and my spirituality—means going through, and sometimes around, the mothering part of me. She is the guardian, the keeper of keys, standing between me and my wild side. If Mama ain't happy, ain't nobody getting *any*.

Popular culture doesn't make shifting gears any easier. It appears to celebrate sexy motherhood, but it's presented as a triumph over nature, an anomaly. The Hot Mom, a tabloid staple, is hot in spite of being a mother, not because of it. The call-outs—BACK

IN A BIKINI! STILL SEXY!—have the sensational ring of a carnival barker. Behold the MILF. She's a super freak.

There are no DILFs. Not because there aren't any lustworthy dads, but because fatherhood is neither here nor there when it comes to sex appeal. If a guy with kids turns you on, there's no reason to act surprised. His body doesn't bear the scars and sags of pregnancy and birth. His sexual organs don't dribble and leak through his clothes. If a new dad shows up with dark circles under his eyes, and stubble on his cheeks, no one whispers that he has let himself go. Unless fatherhood coincides with a career change, he doesn't style himself any differently. I've never caught Patrick standing in front of his closet lamenting that a favorite pair of shoes is no longer practical. He didn't struggle with the conflict between his identity as a loving father and his identity as a sexual man. There is no conflict, psychologically, biologically, or otherwise. Each time he held a new son, his chest puffed out like a preening alpha mountain gorilla. BEHOLD, his body language pronounced.

He thought I was entitled to bear myself with as much triumph. "Your shape is beautiful," he'd tell me. "Womanly."

I discounted it as the raving of a man desperate to get laid, but I was grateful for the kindness. Losing the weight got progressively harder with each kid, and though most of the pounds eventually came off, the skin and muscle never did snap back in place. "How did I look?" I asked Patrick anxiously, on the drive home from an occasion for which I'd braved a slinky dress. "Hot," he said wisely, before blowing it with an ill-considered aside. "There was only that one time when you were slouching a bit, that anyone could see what was really going on down there." "There," meaning my stomach.

I think he thought he was being co-conspiratorial. Maybe he thought the true state of my abdomen was our fun little secret, like not wearing panties.

I almost made him wreck the car. " 'Going on down there'?" I shouted. "Nothing should be going on down there! It's *supposed* to be a static situation. *Verbs* shouldn't come into it."

"I mean," he stammered.

"*Shut up.*" There's such a thing as too much sharing, even within the bonds of matrimony. We drove the rest of the way home in silence, and I became friendly with foundation garments after that. They do a pretty good job of keeping anything from *going* anywhere, though they are hideously expensive, and—no matter how hard you try to reimagine them as fetish wear—decidedly unsexy. But they make my clothed figure look like maybe I don't hate exercise. It felt a little dishonest at first, like false advertising, but it's not as if anyone but Patrick is going to take me home at the end of the evening and find out what is really "going on" down there. It helps keep me faithful. Some cultures require women to reinforce their chastity with long underwear. Some with veils. I have Spanx.

The subterfuge itself doesn't bother me. I've always liked the implements and armature of femininity, and I took them up willingly. I begged my feminist mother to let me wear makeup as soon as I became a teenager. I love cosmetics and perfume. I can hot-roller set my hair in the dark. The brushes, the push-ups, the tanners, and tweezers have always been playthings. A girl's game of dress-up. What I don't like is feeling like I need it, and need more of it, just to look like myself. Or how I think my self should still look. Frankly, it's asking too much of the Spanx.

The baby daughter of one of my girlfriends has magnificently

· 94 ·

plump thighs that everyone within arm's reach is compelled to squeeze and worship. "Why can't it stay that way?" I lamented to her mother at the swimming pool. "Why can't we smile at each other in our bathing suits and be delighted at our jiggles and rolls?"

My friend grinned gamely and pointed to my backside. "Dimples!" she squealed.

Though I know better, there is a residual part of me that goes on believing things will soon return to "normal," including my body. That indefatigable spirit watched the birth of three children, turned around and said, "Whew. Okay, now where was I?" expecting to just pick up where I left off at twenty-nine. It's pitiful, like a coma patient who wakes up and learns her true love didn't wait around. There was a time I could lose five pounds just by thinking about it. That metabolism is MIA. It ran off with my sleep cycle, my hormones, and my sex drive, and before they all split, they stuffed their pockets with collagen and hair pigment. If you see them, call me. I am offering a sizable reward for information leading to their capture and return: 1-800-WHT-THFK.

At least time is an equal opportunity bandit. Men escape the physical ravages of childbearing, but not those of aging. Patrick arrived at midlife six years ahead of me. In as many years as it took my body to host and evict three kids, he went from a skinny guy in his thirties to a not-so-skinny-anymore guy in his forties. The waistband size of his pants finally caught up to his inseam. For a long time, he resisted my suggestions to go up a size, insisting he would soon return to his original proportions. I catch him paused in consternation in front of his closet, or grimacing at the mirror. Instead of puffing out his chest, I see him sucking in his stomach. It's all very familiar. And it's my turn to be kind.

"Sexy," I remark when he wears his new bifocals to read in bed. Persuading him to retire a snug pair of jeans, I tell him, "You were always too thin anyway." I mean all of it. It's true we aren't what we used to be. The window for us ever making a porno has closed. So be it. The stretch marks, dimples, and flab are between him and me, like the years. It's a history we share, one we recite together by touch and sight, know by heart. Like opening a beloved book, creased and dog-eared, for the thousandth time, and skipping straight to your favorite part. I can't imagine having to start over on page one with anyone. There was a time when I didn't necessarily need to catch a person's last name before getting in bed together, let alone know his life story. Now, whenever I hear of someone getting divorced and beginning to date again, I am both fascinated and horrified by the idea, as if I were six years old and just heard about sex for the first time from my best friend's big sister. How does it work, I wonder? Where do people even begin? It was awkward for us to get started after three months of not knowing each other carnally, but at least I could be sure my kids liked this guy.

We were just finding our place when I heard the baby squeak. We had about two minutes before it escalated into a howl, at which point it would breach the sound barrier that envelops the paternal ear. I wondered how to bring things to a hasty conclusion without breaking the mood. "Oops, time's up" seemed, well, anticlimactic. There was a second warning squeak, and inhibition gave way to urgency. I let loose with a litany of pornographic exhortations that caused my inner earth mother to run shrieking to the dark recesses of my conscious brain. As I whispered unspeakable filth into my husband's ear, I stopped worrying about my body's potential for dripping and drooping. I wasn't anxious that the kids would hear the bedsprings creak. Or that the baby would taste the sweat on me when I finally did go nurse him back to sleep.

It was all coming back to me. I skipped straight to my favorite part.

As I got up to fetch the baby, my husband, happy and mussed, reminded me that being a mommy and feeling sexy don't have to be mutually exclusive states of being.

"You are one hot mama," he pronounced, before falling dead asleep.

I drew our baby boy to my breast, where he latched on lustily and noisily. I lay with him and his father in our rumpled bed listening to my men breathing heavy in the night, feeling exalted and adored, goddess of love and milk and all things sweet and salty, sacred and profane.

# 8

# Feast of Sorrow

Wanda died two days after we brought her home. Or maybe it was one day. It took me a while to be certain, since she was nestled among the stems of an aquatic plant that prevented her from floating belly-up to the surface of the goldfish bowl. I was pretty sure it wasn't normal for her to be pointed head-down for so long, but her tail and fins would waft gently in the current of the air filter, and I thought it was possible she was resting, or just disoriented. On Saturday, the morning of Day Three, I reached in and gave the leaves a little shake. Wanda promptly fell upward and assumed the definitive position. I woke Patrick up with the sad news. His preference for disposal of the remains was a private flushing. Less said, the better, was his philosophy as far as the children were concerned.

"Let's not make a big production of this," he suggested, in the rich blended tone of foresight and futility that comes only with years of marriage.

"What are you talking about?" I said, with feeling. "Of course, we're having a funeral—this is how children learn to deal with death. *This*," I declared with hyperbole, "is why we let them have pets." Moved by my own case, I began to sing the chorus from the "Circle of Life," but his head was already under the pillow.

Men don't know how to deal with their grief, I thought sadly, scooping Wanda into a plastic baggie and stashing her temporarily in the vegetable crisper. I was determined it would be different for my boys. When they woke up, I gave it to them straight: Wanda hadn't made it; she had died. They were mildly curious. Where was she now, they wanted to know, inspecting the goldfish bowl. I explained that while her body was with the carrots in the refrigerator, her spirit was surely swimming with God.

I announced we were having a funeral with full honors, and that someone would have to dig a hole. My oldest, six years old at the time, was enthusiastic about this part, excavating a large hole in the lawn beneath our maple tree. He also helped me bind two Popsicle sticks together with kitchen twine for a cross.

"Wanda," I read aloud, inscribing the grave marker with a permanent felt-tip pen, "2005."

I capped the pen. "Now it's time to get Wanda."

At this point, the sexton lost muster and looking askance, said he'd rather go back inside and watch television, thanks. I praised his work and let him go. His four-year-old brother, who during the digging and construction phase had been gathering dandelions for a memorial spray, followed me raptly to the refrigerator to see what would happen next.

The deceased was holding up rather well, considering. I lifted the baggie out, and we observed her in silence for a moment, before proceeding on our way to the front yard as pallbearers. Under the canopy of red maple leaves, I unzipped the bag and poured Wanda into her final resting place. My son helped shovel dirt over the grave with a small garden trowel, and laid his bouquet of yellow flowers at the base of the cross. I turned to the prayer I had chosen from the board book edition of *A Child's Book of Prayers*.

"Dear Father, please hear and bless thy beasts and singing birds," I read. "And guard with special tenderness small things that have no words. Amen."

I closed the prayer book and smiled serenely at my son, lesson accomplished. I was not prepared to see his fathomless blue eyes brimming with tears. His small shoulders sagged as he collapsed against my leg, sobbing.

"Oh, sweetheart," I exclaimed, falling to my knees to comfort him. I was horrified. What kind of sick, morbid sadist was I, anyway? How many years of therapy would it take to recover from a mother who interrupts Saturday-morning cartoons to make you carry your cold, dead pet to the front yard and shovel dirt onto it? My husband was right—I take things too far.

As usual, I had arrived at one extreme by way of a nonstop flight from another. Earlier in my career as mother, I took pains to avoid a direct discussion of mortality with my kids. They had just arrived here, after all. Why spoil the fun right away with the dark and terrible truth? I thought it was better to let them down gently. Whenever possible, I evaded the subject of death.

"Mommy, where do chicken nuggets come from?"

"The grocery store. Ketchup?"

Or I waxed euphemistic. "That bird left his body here and went to fly in heaven," I'd say, as we paused over a feathered corpse lying in the gutter.

My illusion that I could or should shield them from life's big spoiler ended abruptly one night as I was tucking my eldest son in bed. I was telling him a story about my father.

"Where *is* Poppy?" my son asked pointedly.

I smiled sadly. "He went to live with God, baby."

My son propped his head up and looked at me with a kind but resolute expression, like a psychotherapist about to get down to business. He touched my arm.

"Do you mean he's *dead*, Mom?" he asked, gently.

In my momnipotence, I sometimes forget that my kids came fully assembled. When they were infants, I'd marvel over their tiny ears, how intricately formed they were, pink and golden like the inside of a conch. They were miraculous to me. And humbling, because I can't draw an ear, much less take credit for making one. I lose sight of that from time to time, and delude myself into thinking I'm the *auteur* of their experience, when actually, I mainly work in catering. They don't need me directing, feeding them their lines. They get it. The script for life and death, grief and joy, is written on their DNA.

As I knelt in the dirt around Wanda's grave, my weeping son clasped to my chest, my grandiosity dissolved. He knew his part. Not in my little production, but in the theater of life. His mourning was both authentic and appropriate, and all that was required of me was to honor it. "Let's have some juice," I suggested, brushing his sandy brown hair from his eyes. We walked up the steps to the front porch and sat at the boys' little table. I brought out the whole jug of orange juice and two plastic tumblers. I thought we could both use a drink.

"To Wanda," I said, raising my glass.

To life, I thought. The bitter and the sweet.

I wanted to teach my kids about grief without exposing them to it. There was just so much death around us during our children's first years, I was afraid of the shadow it might cast over them. My mother-in-law passed away four months before our oldest son was born. My father-in-law followed her less than five years later. In between, there was a nine-month stretch during which my father, both my grandmothers, and our dog died, and exploding in the center of that year's cold heart, its atomic nucleus, September 11. It felt like the end of time.

Though it sounds like something straight out of a cheesy country-and-western song, the dog took it over the top. Bailey was my Chesapeake Bay retriever, an eighty-pound lap dog I'd adopted the week after we got married. She drowned before my eyes, in a lake in the country, catching sticks. There was no one around but me and the kids, and the baby could crawl, fast. I didn't dare leave him and my two-year-old on the shore while I jumped in to rescue her, so I watched helplessly as she thrashed and rolled in the water. Some people on the far shore heard my shouts and came running, hauled her out, and revived her long enough for me to get her to the emergency vet clinic, but it was too late. The call came in the middle of the night that she was gone. Patrick brought home her collar and the X-ray image of her waterlogged lungs, a dark cloud passing over her heart, moving into mine.

I could extract some meaning from the other losses, if only as an end to suffering, but Bailey's death mocked those inferences with its gratuitousness. Chesapeakes are bred for swimming—they have webbed feet and waterproof coats. Something had caused her to take on a little water—a stroke, maybe, or exhaustion—and in no time at all, she was sinking. I saw how quickly she lost her sense of which way was up, and I knew I was also danger-ously close to the tipping point. Your center of gravity changes when a loved one dies. Part of your life goes with them, so you no longer stand with your full weight on this side, each loss inclining you a little more toward death. I was beginning to list. I tucked my children under my arms, and I pushed off from the silt-bottom sadness with everything I had, diverting my grief into compart-ments I had sealed off a long time ago.

My unwept tears for my grandfather sloshed around in one of them. He was the first person close to me who died. I was eight years old, and he was the god of my small heaven until cancer took him from me. He went into the hospital for a while, then he came home to his bedroom. I watched my parents, uncles, and aunts coming and going from there for weeks, before I was called to go see him, all by myself. I was scared as I walked down the dim hallway toward the door. I had been told he was dying, and I grasped the word, but not the reality. I knew dimly that it meant he was going away and not coming back, but when he saw me, and began to cry, I understood fully. He didn't *want* to die. He was scared, too. I ran out of the room, terror stricken, and ashamed of myself for abandoning him.

I turned to the god of my grandfather's heaven, and I began to pray in earnest for the first time in my life. Not for a miracle—I knew that would be asking too much—but for one small mercy: *When Poppy dies, don't let me cry.* I prayed those words over and over. I suppose I thought if I didn't cry, I might not hurt. Or maybe the shock of seeing my grandfather break down made me fearful of tears. But that's hand-tinting the picture with an adult brush, guessing at the true colors. I don't remember the reasons, only the urgency. The prayer was answered. I didn't cry when I heard the news, or saw my grandfather in his coffin, or walked behind him to the grave. I was proud of keeping it together. I felt very grown up, though the actual grown-ups were weeping freely. In a world that could apparently take anything from me, at any time, I at least had mastered my emotions.

As kids, we make those kinds of internal errors in navigation, deviations that are slight in the beginning, but widen tangentially as we grow, taking us a little further off course each year. My attitude toward grief became very skewed. For years, I felt about crying the way most people feel about throwing up. I'd really rather not, even if I did feel better afterward. If I had to cry, I did it alone and in private, and there had to be a good reason for it, like death or divorce. I was afraid that if I started crying, I might not be able to stop. Other people's crying made me very uncomfortable. It was like watching them vomit. I'd avert my eyes and hand them a tissue.

I've tried to get better about it since having children. I want the boys to know that sorrow is natural and acceptable. I can tell them, but I have trouble showing them. My tendency is still to hide when I need to cry. I go to the bathroom and turn on the faucet to mask the sobbing, or slip out the back door to sit on the steps. I wait for the redness of my eyes and face to settle down before I reemerge, worried that my tears will frighten them, or that I'll have to explain whatever it is that's the matter. I don't want to have to tell them that awful things happen to people, or that their parents are capable of hurting each other sometimes, or that someone who isn't done with living can die.

But grief seeps in anyway, especially during the holidays, when the absence of our parents feels most acute, and the lengthening nights invite melancholy. We light the Advent wreath to mark off the time. Three weeks in, we come to the pink candle. Anglicans say the color is for "joyful anticipation," but I borrow from my Catholic roots, and claim it for Mary, for the mother. The candlelight kindles storytelling. We linger in its glow after supper, and Patrick tells the boys about Christmases past, years when his family filled and overflowed the house that belonged to his grandmother, long gone. As he enumerates kin, the boys' eyes grow wide. It's hard for them to imagine. They don't know the kind of family gatherings we did as children.

Baby boy, at three and a half, perceives the void outlined by these stories. He climbs into my lap, and with both hands pulls my face toward his. "Who grandfather's name called?" he whispers.

"Al," I tell him. "And Patrick. Poppy and PawPaw."

"Who grandmother's name?"

"Nanny."

"Who other grandmother's name called?"

"Honey."

"Honey," he repeats.

Old grief is a cunning street robber. It can pick your pocket slyly in a crowd, without you noticing your joy is gone. Or it ambushes you straight on, out of nowhere, steel to your gut. Your knees hit the ground and you're breathless.

I gaze into the flame of the rose candle. Not in joyful anticipation, but with thought for La Virgen María de los Dolores, Virgin Mary of Sorrows. Patrick and I spent a season of Lent in Mexico, where a fiesta is dedicated to the sorrowful mother, and people open their homes to display elaborate house altars in her honor, adorned with wheatgrass and bitter oranges.

I was in fresh, raw grief at the time, mourning the end of my first marriage. It was the kind of sadness that makes every breath an effort, a decision. It sounds very romantic to say I ran off to Mexico with my lover, but the truth is, I spent most of my days there in a fog. The Night of the Altars pierced it. Sorrow and loss were allowed. I wanted to gather all the oranges into my arms, bite them through their skins. I began to understand that the pain wouldn't let go of me unless I clasped it first.

I sometimes think we haven't been able to gather in the pain of losing our parents. As they were going, our children were coming. There hasn't been time or space. In the case of Patrick's parents, I'm not sure we've ever come out of shock. Even my dad's death, more expected, still seems unreal. My mother and sister experience his absence nearly every day, but I only encounter it when I visit. I remember riding in the back of a car with my sister in front of me on the way to Mom's from the airport a few years ago. My sister was saying, "When Dad died . . . ," and I could hear my own voice inside my head, asking *"What* did she say?"

My husband doesn't have the geographic disconnect, but he also manages to get around the gaping hole. We don't visit Patrick's parents' graves, a half-hour drive. We almost never get together with his brother's family, although our relationship with them is genuinely warm. Apart from Christmas cards exchanged with a steadfast few, we don't see or hear from relatives or friends of his parents. Patrick's never been back to the house his father sold soon after his mother died. It's as if the entire space they carved out in the world simply closed over.

Every year, my children's schools have a Grandparents' Day,

and every year I have to scramble to come up with a substitute grandparent for each of them. Once, the best I could do was get a co-worker they'd never met. The schools insist I come up with somebody. I lamented the situation to a friend's ninety-four-year-old mother once, half hoping she would take the bait. She had outlived two husbands and a daughter.

"Well, honey," she said, smiling, and patting my arm, "that's just the way it is."

She was right. I decided we needed to accept reality. The reality, I told my boys, is that they have only one grandparent, and she lives 2,500 miles away, and it's too bad, but Grandparents' Day is probably always going to be a drag for them because of it.

It's just the way it is. Sorrow and loss are allowed.

I have to remember her words when Patrick describes for the boys how deeply the presents would be piled under his tree. *Oh, don't tell them that,* I think. I don't want my children to feel lack. But they do lack, and it's not in presents. It's in three wonderful people who would have loved them unconditionally, and indulged them shamelessly, the way only grandparents can do. Even my youngest, the only child to never meet any of them, understands that some of his family are missing, and misses them.

I have to let him. Even if it means I have to miss them, too.

# 9

# For Richer, for Poorer

I never used to pay attention to foreclosure notices. They were just inscrutable boxes of black-and-white text I had to flip past to get to a more interesting section of the newspaper. I slow down when I see them now, as I might do if I were passing headstones in a graveyard. I'm aware there are names and dates buried in the legalese: a street, an address. A home. Sometimes I'll stop and read them. The names are often followed by the words "husband and wife."

I wonder how they're doing, if they'll make it.

It wasn't that long ago that my husband and I were the ones facing foreclosure, hanging off a cliff by our well-gnawed fingernails. I know the exhaustion and terror of staring into that abyss. It's hard on the soul, and it's hell on a marriage. It's tempting to assume that people who fall on hard times have brought it upon themselves, through recklessness or greed. But every financial disaster is disastrous in its own way—easy enough to see where the downward spiral ends, harder to sort out where it began.

The year our last child was born, Patrick left a twenty-year career in corporate advertising to open his own design studio. Other people on the verge of such a leap might have gotten all their ducks in a row first: formulated a business plan, banked a year's worth of living expenses.

We've never been other people. There was no plan. Our ducks tend to be free-range. We'd chased after them a few times—like running off to Mexico early in our courtship to live until our money ran out, then coming back to the States to start over with nothing but our clothes and an antique Mercury Comet, powder blue and chrome. "Fortune favors the bold" was our motto.

When we married, we vowed to keep following our bliss. But after our kids came, Patrick's wistful notion of working for himself kept getting deferred. "When the children are all in school," I'd tell him. Or, "When we've saved enough money." And then, "When we're out of debt." When it feels safe to abandon a predictable paycheck, matching contributions to a 401(k), group health insurance, and paid vacation, that's when. That day never came. Patrick kept the lid on his growing unhappiness until it began to leak out messily; then he and his job broke up.

At the time, my income as a part-time administrative assistant barely covered groceries. It was just something on the side, a foothold in the grown-up world. The job that mattered most to me was being home with our three small children. I thought it was the thing that mattered most to Patrick also—a noble reason to put up with an unsatisfactory situation for a few more years, at least. I was angry, disappointed, and frightened when he came to the end of his rope.

But I could also see how deeply unhappy my husband had become, and how long he'd been trying to hide it. His career as a hired hand in a small market was at a creative dead end. Freelancing from our home would give him the variety and autonomy he was longing for, and allow him to spend more time with our kids. We had a little bit of savings, and Patrick had twenty years' worth of contacts in the business. I was willing to give it a chance. As the saying goes, when the students are ready, the teacher will appear. Ours was a financial adviser named Linda. A friend recommended her, assuring us that even one session would be an hour and $75 well spent. Linda listened to our hopes and fears, reviewed our numbers, looked us straight in the eye, and told us in her no-bull New England accent, "You can do this."

Although Patrick had talked over the years about striking out on his own, I had frankly underestimated the motivating power of independence. The husband I had feared was too laid-back to chase clients methodically and determinedly sought work, and work came. But his business tends to be one of feast or famine, subject to seasonal cycles, economic conditions, and chance. Months sometimes passed between checks; sometimes, between jobs.

"Why didn't we go to med school?" I said to Patrick when my son asked why he couldn't buy his school lunch instead of packing it every day. "What were we thinking?"

Linda gave us perspective for the long haul. "Look," she'd say, when our confidence wavered, "most start-ups don't show any profit at all in the first few years. You guys are making your living from this right out of the gate."

Well, barely. But it helped to hear it. Besides her sheer faith in our abilities, and helping us budget, Linda's most valuable contribution during our start-up year was to remind us that we had choices. "You could rent out a room in your house," she pointed out. "You could sell it. You can enroll the kids in public school instead of paying private tuition."

She was right. We did have choices. But we were trying not to exercise the tough ones. I, especially, was still clinging to the infrastructure of salaried life. We may have lived paycheck to paycheck, but at least there was a paycheck, and we knew when to expect it. As much I as prided myself on being resourceful, I never wanted to be the poster girl for frugal living. I enjoy material comforts as much as the next person. I'd been looking at sharing a car and hand-me-downs as short-term pain for long-term gain. Packing lunches and clipping coupons felt thrifty. The idea of making drastic changes to our living space or the children's education was traumatic. The school is special, we explained. Our home is sacred.

Linda challenged us to rethink all our assumptions. "What are you waiting for?" she asked, when she learned I had put writing on the vocational back burner.

I found I didn't have a good answer for that, since it was something I could do from home. I had the uncomfortable awareness that I had been using my kids as a shield between my dream and me. I kept my paying job, but I also began writing again. My first fee—$100 for a guest commentary in a newspaper—felt like a cool million.

At the end of our first year in business, we got a pleasant surprise: We weren't too far behind our income from Patrick's corporate job the year before. Cost-cutting measures filled in some of the gap. We closed the rest with savings withdrawals and credit cards. Meantime, Patrick and I were reveling in the novelty of being at home together every day.

The second year proved to be a different story. Nearly every month, there was a point at which we thought the last job had gone out the door. No one would ever give us another dime. And then suddenly Patrick would be deluged and working seventy-two-hour stretches. Remind me how this is less stressful than agency work, I was tempted to ask at those times. Remind me about all the togetherness, I wanted to say, when he was working morning to night and I was feeling nostalgic for Monday to Friday, eight to five.

We survived those months one last-minute reprieve after another. Disaster would loom, and a check would appear at the fifty-ninth minute of the eleventh hour. I was frustrated, fatigued, and furious at the zero-sum-ness of it all. Always just enough. Always just in time. I was sick of *just*. We were living retroactively, unable to get enough traction to get caught up, much less ahead. The question of affording school tuition for the next year became moot. I wrote the headmistress, informing her we'd have to withdraw. She steered us to scholarship funds that would fully supplement the financial aid we already received.

On registration day, my third-grader saw the brochure for after-school chess classes and asked me if he could sign up. "I don't have money for that today," I said, in the most neutral tone I could muster. A smartly dressed mother at the sign-up table turned to look at me. A moment later, another parent walked up beside me, the mother of the kid whose used social studies book I had bought for my son. In what would have been a comedy of errors if it hadn't been so embarrassing, the check I had written for it had bounced, and then the check I had written to cover that had bounced. The book wound up costing me an arm and a leg after all the fees had been paid. It's expensive to be poor.

Not one of these events in isolation would have fazed me. I'm okay with telling my kids when we can't afford something. As my friend who works in a posh boutique assures me, even wealthy people bounce checks sometimes. But all together, it was just too much. I cried more that year than I had in all the other years we'd been married. I worried we were failing our kids.

We'd been meeting with Linda less regularly, since we could no longer afford to pay cash, and I hated to take advantage of her willingness to run us a tab. When I put in an SOS call, she insisted we come in that day.

Ironically, in spite of our day-to-day crises, the big picture was looking good. Patrick's client base was growing; my writing was getting picked up. To quit now would be to throw away all that promise. "Now is not the time to take your eyes off the ball," Linda reminded us. "Let's go over all of your choices."

The "choices" now were very simple: declaring bankruptcy or selling the house. Linda calmly outlined the pros and cons of each. Everything was on the table now. My husband and I tiptoed around it gingerly, the way we walked around each other.

Only from the safety of Linda's office could Patrick say aloud what he thought we should do. He had asked me to come out on this limb with him, and he knew there were days I was close to pushing him off, when I wished he would just grow up, get a real job. *Rescue me.*

"I think maybe it's become harder to hang on to the house than it would be to let it go," Patrick said quietly.

Easy for you to say, I felt like shouting. This was all your stupid idea anyway. But I knew Linda would never let me get away with it. Choices, she'd say. Decisions. It was time for us to make one. Patrick was open to either selling the house or rebooting our debt load by filing for bankruptcy. Whatever it would take to turn us around, forward facing. I wanted to explore refinancing our house first. Our credit was shot, but we had built quite a bit of equity. All of us agreed it was worth a try.

It's nice to think, before life really tests you, that you'll be the couple who exemplify unity and grace under pressure. I would like to tell you we are that couple. But the truth is, the navigation of life's more harrowing storms has not always been accomplished using our indoor voices. On a good day, I was proud of my husband for striking out on his own, and proud of myself for being able to take the leap of faith with him. On a good day, one of us could always find a way to make the other smile. "Got to keep you in the lifestyle to which you've lowered your expectations," he'd say with a wink and a grin, when I'd chide him about working long hours. On a good day, I knew that our marriage did not depend on the score on our credit report.

The Tuesday before Thanksgiving 2007 was not a good day.

The fall quarter had been unusually slow. Patrick made only a few hundred dollars the entire month of October. A client who owed him thousands more was MIA. Our attempt to refinance our home had hit a brick wall. We were spiraling down. The only avenue left was to try and sell quickly, ahead of foreclosure. In the meantime, there was the immediate future and the holiday season to get through. I knew we would have to swallow our pride and reach out. That morning, I drove past a man on the freeway holding a cardboard sign. COULD USE A LITTLE HELP, it said. I had ten dollars in my purse and I didn't know where the next ten dollars was coming from. I was on the opposite side of the road. It would make a good story to say I turned around and gave him half of what I had, but I didn't. I borrowed the words of his sign and hung them on my heart instead.

We could use a little help, I e-mailed my mom and a family friend through tears. I was exhausted, embarrassed, and afraid. "If we lose our home," I said to Patrick balefully, "I don't know if I can forgive you."

Patrick, already haunted by the thought of failing to provide for his family, bent his head and walked outside to sit on the porch and brood. All night, my bitter words hung in the air. I thought it would make me feel better if I could point my finger at someone and say, "You did this, now you fix it." It didn't. I had the sick feeling I had cashed in something precious for something very cheap.

The next day, the eve of Thanksgiving, I got up early and considered our blessings. We had family and friends who would not let us go homeless or hungry. We had three healthy and happy sons whom we hoped we were buffering from the worst of our anxiety. We'd had promising signs that our respective careers would flourish if we could just pull away from the whirlpool our reverse cash flow had created.

And we had each other. Once, that had been all I ever wanted.

"Meet me a little bit of the way," Patrick said to me, when he was living in Mexico, and I was frozen in fear and indecision at the opposite corner of the continent. "Just a little bit," he repeated. "I'll come all the rest of the way to meet you."

I packed a bag, got on a bus, and met him a few hundred miles from where I put down the phone. He came the other few thousand. The best part of my life was everything that happened after. Surely, after ten years of marriage I could find it in me to meet him more than just a little bit of the way.

Patrick came downstairs with the same stricken look I'd put on his face the day before. I took his hand in mine; felt the innumerable, tiny scratches etched into his wedding band. If I counted them up, like the rings of a tree, would they tell the years?

"I'm so sorry," I said to him. "We can let go of this house. But not each other."

Soon after the Christmas decorations came down, the FOR SALE sign went up. That was a Thursday. The SOLD sign went up Saturday. Sunday, we went out and picked out our new house. We are people who routinely spend an hour driving around trying to decide where to spend thirty-five bucks on supper. By extrapolation, a set of back-to-back real estate transactions should have taken us a year. But I guess if you include all the hand-wringing leading up to the decision, it sort of did.

I can hardly tell you now what that was all about, but I've since come to believe that houses have minds of their own. They choose who comes and goes. As it turned out, our house had been making eyes at another woman for some time. She lived a few blocks away, and had been in love with it for years. She and her husband had looked at countless listings, but none of them turned out to be what they were looking for. "What *are* you looking for?" a visitor asked her one evening, out of curiosity.

"I'll show you," she said, taking her by our house, where the realtor's sign had just been posted. Patrick heard the story when the buyer came over with the inspector, after we accepted the offer. Blood could have been pouring from the walls, he said, and she wouldn't have been deterred. But the walls oozed nothing but the character and soul of a fine old house that had been our home for ten years. Under its roof, we had become a family, the good and bad times layered together like plaster and lathe. It was a part of our history, and we were part of its. I cried when I locked the door and drove away, but I was at peace knowing it would be loved.

On the other side of the paperwork, there was a new house for us. The day after our bid was accepted, we took the kids back over for another look, and saw that the seller's truck was in the driveway.

"I think it would be nice for you guys to meet," our real estate agent said. Patrick got out of the car ahead of me, and I stayed behind a moment to unload the boys. When I looked up, Patrick was hugging a strange man.

Well, that's just inappropriate, I thought. I started to walk over, slightly embarrassed over my husband's low personal boundaries, and extended my hand.

"Kyran."

"Charles?"

He was an old friend we had lost track of years before, and it was his childhood home we were buying from his elderly mother. She had lived in it long enough to raise two children, bury one of them, and be widowed twice. If I added up all my angst over letting go of our first home, and multiplied it by a half-century of love and loss, I might have a faint appreciation for what she was going through. Charles was overjoyed to be able to tell his mother that the house wouldn't go to strangers. We have since had her back for visits, and she has regaled the kids with eyewitness accounts of farm animals walking down our suburban street.

As I get older, I get softer toward refrigerator magnet theology. You know, "God never closes a door without opening a window," that sort of thing. I swear, the minute we let go of everything we'd been fighting so hard to keep, whatever had been stuck came unstuck, and opportunity came pouring in. Jobs that had been stalled for months resumed. Checks arrived for invoices that had been all but written off. You could almost hear the "pop." One thing after another fell into place.

We were lucky to buy a house at all, considering the state of our credit, but that didn't keep this beggar from being choosy. Our first house came with a long list of to-do's that rolled over into a perpetual list of make-do's, and I'd be damned if we were moving into another fixer-upper. We were downsizing from a large house in a fashionable neighborhood to a smaller house in an up-and-coming one, and the differential not only afforded us the down payment we needed to leverage a new mortgage, it gave us a small fund for renovations and furnishings. As far as I was concerned, it had to be fait accompli before we moved in. We packed our belongings, Tetris-like, into a portable storage pod and set up housekeeping in a tiny condominium nearby, while I played general contractor.

A renovation project is the suburban vision quest. As a test of endurance and character, it's hard to beat. Through ours, I made some surprising self-discoveries: I have an excellent eye for color, a preference for modern design, and a minimum personal space requirement that exceeds an eight-hundred-square-foot apartment with one bathroom. I have seen into my own soul, and it is thoroughly bourgeois.

This contradicts my personal mythology. Everyone has stories they tell themselves about themselves, and one of mine is that I am a gypsy at heart. Like most myths, mine has distant, historical origins. I lost two homes before I let the last one go, one to fire, and one to divorce. I understand very well that the essential things are always replaceable, and the irreplaceable things are never essential. But after being settled in one place for ten years, it wasn't easy to be rootless again. It turns out I was more of a stray than a rover. When I find shelter, I cling to it. I dig in deep.

We were only moving a few miles, but it felt like we had set sail for the Antipodes. Leaving home is leaving home, no matter the mileage. Whether your front door opens to rolling fields or concrete and asphalt, over the course of a decade, you become intimate with the land you live on. It's the kind of physical familiarity you develop with your mate and your children, the cellular knowledge of their scent, their hair, the body's topography, the way your hand wanders absently along the beloved's vertebrae, your fingertips like small hounds on a knobby trail, stopping at the tailbone, muzzles pressed to the base of a tree. *This place. I know this place.* I had that intimacy with our quarter acre on Spruce Street. After ten years of gardening, raking, picking up toys, bringing out trash, letting out dogs, calling in kids, I knew every root and leaf, every shadow and season. It was weedy, as untidy as a little boy's unbrushed hair, but I loved it in detail and in particular. The scarlet of the Japanese maple at a certain hour, on a certain day in November, when the sun hit at a certain angle. The golden green of a patch of moss behind the spirea hedge in winter when the canes were laid bare. The exact weight of the back garden gate, laden under tentacled ivy.

I knew that place. It was home.

We thought we'd be in transit for a month. It stretched to two. It was hardest on the kids, who had been so caught up in packing and picking colors for their new rooms, the reality of leaving their nest was slow to hit them. Each one had to come around to it in his own way, in his own time. One night, my preschooler suddenly got busy rounding up shoes and toys.

"It's time to go!" he announced jubilantly.

"Go where, sweetie?" I asked with considerably less energy. It was nearly ten o'clock—our bedtime routines were as disrupted as everything else.

"To our old house!"

He said it with such joy and eagerness, it killed me to break it to him that, no, we couldn't go back to the old house. He fell to pieces.

"But I want my old room," he wept.

Me too, I thought. We hadn't shared such close quarters since the oldest boys were babies. Everybody's last nerve was underfoot, waiting to be stepped on. A few nights later, I sent my eldest son to his room after being contradicted one too many times. He silently fumed at me with a rage I had nearly forgotten a child could feel for a parent. I gave him a minute or two to himself and then went up to talk to him. He kept his back turned and his arms crossed over his chest, palms grasping opposite shoulders, like he always does when he is hurting. I talked to his back for a few minutes about parental respect, and cultivating a positive attitude, and the place of civil disobedience in a benign dictatorship such as our own. He was impenetrable.

I turned the lecture off. "C'mere," I said, and managed to coax his armadillo-rolled body next to mine. "Look, I know it's hard right now to be living in between. I know you are probably missing home . . ."

At the word "home," he began to cry, the heaving, rushing sobs that come from grief that's been gathering deep in the gut. I gathered him up into my arms and told him the things I missed about our house: watching him and his brothers climb the Japanese maple, the hidden places in the yard where they dug and played. I promised him that he would soon be climbing the trees in our new yard, digging new holes. I halfheartedly began the speech that "home is where the heart is," then abandoned it, because it's bullshit. I've been uprooted enough myself to know that sometimes home is a physical place you need desperately to get back to. Tell a banked fish that home is where the heart is. So I shut up, and held him and stroked his sandy brown hair until it was over. Then I told him to fill the tub and take a nice long bubble bath, bedtime be damned.

A few weeks later, finally, the last coat of varnish on the floors was dry enough for sock feet. We flung open the door, threw our sleeping bags down on the bedroom carpet, and ordered pizza, five happy campers. We were home.

Heightening our sensation of having left the known world behind us was the fact that we brought hardly any of our old furniture along. Most of it had been handed down to us or bought at yard sales and thrift markets, and was crappy and cheap even when it was brand-new. The week before we moved out, we hauled it by batches to the corner of the yard, posting notices on the Internet for freecyclers. I'd lie in bed at night, listening to the cars pull up and the whispers of people picking over the junk pile. In the morning, it was all magically gone. I felt like a kid who comes downstairs Christmas morning and sees that Santa has eaten the cookies.

Letting go is always hard, but starting over is something I do well. Only things we felt good about were allowed in our new space. If it wasn't loved or useful, it couldn't come over the threshold. We met that criteria with sale and outlet items, with the exception of one true luxury: a coveted set of designer chairs. I'd seen them in a magazine, and predicated our entire paint scheme on their red-orange color, but at the last minute, I didn't know if I could go through with the splurge. We were working with a modest budget by middle-class standards, but I was fighting a rising tide of anxiety. After living on the edge for so long, anything above the lowest tier of the survival pyramid felt like wild extravagance. Scarcity does what its root implies: it scars. I considered substituting some cheaper chairs, just for now. We'd get the good ones someday. But the thought depressed me. How many years had we spent living in "just for now"? When would someday ever arrive?

Then Linda stopped by with a housewarming gift. By then, she was our dear friend as well as financial adviser, but I showed her around as if it were an audit, justifying every new furnishing, each improvement, describing how awful the old sofa was—so bad even the freecyclers wouldn't take it. When we got to Patrick's office, she admired his new desk.

"What were you using before?" she asked. Sheepishly, we pointed to a tiny pine table that had been repurposed as a stand for the kids' computer. It wasn't even practical for that, and was destined for the curb as soon as a real desk could be delivered.

Linda let loose with one of her wonderful Yankee guffaws. "And you've paid the mortgage and the bills working from THAT for two years??? Jesus Christ!"

Jesus Christ, he really did.

I grinned and gestured to my battered laptop on a nearby table. The keyboard letters had worn off, and several of the keys were stuck. "Would you believe I've been writing all this time without a q, a, z, numeral one, or exclamation point?"

Linda, not for the first or last time, looked at me with that look that said thank God there's still a chance I can help you, and asked, "How is that possible?"

I showed how I'd learned to copy and paste the missing keystrokes from a clipboard application. "I don't use q and z much, and I don't even like exclamation points," I explained. "But not having an 'a' *is* kind of a pain in the ass."

Laughter must be the soul's chiropractor. It has a way of realigning all the pinched and twisted parts inside. I ordered the chairs I wanted, arranging them around our glass dining room table beneath Pernod-yellow walls, and every morning when I drink my first cup of coffee in one of them, I feel like I'm sitting at Someday.

It's almost impossible to extract meaning from hardship without employing hackneyed clichés. There was a point that year where if I heard another variation on "That which does not kill us makes us stronger," I was going to scream. Sometimes, that which does not kill us can beat us up and leave us in a ditch. So I hesitate to bring up gratitude, because I know there is someone reading this who is in that ditch today, who'd like to tell me what to do with my gratitude. But there's no way around it. There is nothing like fear for distorting perspective, and nothing like gratitude for restoring it. I'm not talking about the false gratitude that denies that you or anyone else is suffering. Nor the shadowy kind that depends on the truism that somebody, somewhere, is always worse off than you, nor the timid thankfulness that doesn't dare ask more from life than basic survival. I mean really appreciating what is in front of you right now, even if you don't know if you can count on it tomorrow.

"I have everything I need today" became the mantra that brought us through that hard year. Even when we couldn't quite believe it, it never failed to be true. Gratitude still brings us through the rough spots today, when a job is slow to pay or an unexpected expense depletes our modest emergency savings. In the middle of some anxious weeks last year, I walked into my husband's office and peered at him over his computer screen. "Hey," I said.

His eyes looked tired. He'd been working double-time to get us over the hump. I could see his shoulders hunched visibly higher than usual. But he smiled.

"Hey," he said. "How are you doing?" I knew he meant, "How are we doing?" I had just come from the mailbox. Nothing yet. Our big monthly debt-reduction payment had just come out of our checking account. It was down to the three-figure mark, and our mortgage payment was coming due next week.

I reached over the screen and ran my finger along the worry line in my true love's forehead, as if I could smooth it over. It was so much deeper now than it was over a decade ago when we traded all those blithe promises. I had no clue then how poor, how sick, how awful we could sometimes be. Nor any idea how rich, how strong, and how good. For that matter, I still didn't.

Life can get better, it can get worse. It will probably do both. "I have everything I need today," I told him.

I could see in his sleepy eyes that we both did. We still do.

10.

# The Rearview

E ver since I've had kids of my own, I've been subjecting my mother to random fact-checks over the telephone.

"Did you steal the good stuff out of our trick-or-treat bags?"

"Yes."

"Did you pretend to be listening when you weren't?"

"Yes."

"Did you feel like you knew what you were doing most of the time?"

"No."

It's like conducting an exit interview with God. I know there are other ways, besides having children, that people come to terms with their parents' fallibility, but most involve steep hourly fees. I just have long-distance charges.

Parenthood comes with a rearview mirror. At every new turn, you glance into it and line up what you know now, as a parent, with what you believed then, as a child. You hear your father's words coming out of your mouth, or you flash back to your mother at your exact age, and it hits you all over again that *you* are the grown-up, the person in charge. You're the one who is supposed to know things. You remember how safe you felt in the backseat of the family car at night when you were a kid, watching the raindrops shiver and roll down the side window. Now it's you in the driver's seat, white-knuckled at the wheel, praying that all four tires stay on the road. You don't know shit. And neither, you realize, did your parents.

Mercifully, enlightenment comes in stages. Most of us start down the moccasin mile with minor failures of omniscience and build up to the bigger misses gradually. In the early years, you even get magical fall guys to take the blame. Our tooth fairy, for example, is notoriously unreliable.

"What, *again??*" I exclaim on mornings I am presented with an unredeemed tooth on an open palm. "It's the second night in a row! What is *wrong* with that freaking tooth fairy?"

As far as my kids know, the tooth fairy is a drunk, whose operating funds are either tied to a wildly variable interest rate or the racetrack. I can live with that. The magical beings I grew up with also tended to deviate from the official script. I was twenty years old before I discovered that most other children weren't leaving rum for Santa on Christmas Eve, which went a long way toward explaining some of his more memorable lapses in wish fulfillment.

Everyone's childhood disappointments run the gamut between

trivial and traumatic, but it's especially vivid when Santa lets you down. I was nine the year I asked him to bring me a Ken doll. Malibu Ken, Hawaiian Ken, Superstar Ken—I didn't care. Just a Ken, to go with my Barbies, which in my home fell under the same classification as junk food and television: empty pursuits to be indulged sparingly. I only had two, Ballerina and Superstar. You couldn't really count the Bionic Woman, a big-boned and flat-footed gal who towered awkwardly over them by a full inch. They shunned her, and she lived out her days as a recluse under the bed.

The girls had nothing to wear but the clothes they had on their backs the day they arrived. They had no Corvette, no camper, no pony, no dream house. I thought a man around the place would brighten things up. They could at least go dancing and have threesomes.

Barbie deprivation doesn't exactly count as trauma, but that didn't keep me from holding it over my mother's head for years, using it as an excuse for all kinds of girly excesses, including frosted highlights, tanning beds, and vapid boyfriends. To the conscientious few who still wring their hands over Barbie's place in their daughter's toy box and developing body image, I say give in to it. Barbie is the modern-day Venus of Willendorf: stylized, exaggerated, and unable to stand. She represents an aspect of femininity that must be held for a time, literally and symbolically. So she has freakish proportions and no nipples. You think paleo-lithic moms worried that their little girls would grow up feeling something was wrong with them because they had distinct facial features and the Venus of Willendorf didn't? You bet they did. But Santa came through anyway.

Which is more than I can say he did for me on December 25,

1978, when I awoke to find "Chuck and His 4 Outfits" waiting for me under the tree.

Chuck was a squat and swarthy fellow made of thin hollow plastic, not the beefy solid vinyl of a real Mattel man. His four outfits did not make him a fashion doll. His clothes were the uniforms of manual labor: among them, a red-and-black-checked flannel jacket and a blue work shirt that could transition easily between the bowling lane and the prison machine shop. He didn't come in a proper box with a window, just a cellophane bag that was made to hang off a metal rod in the dollar section of the store, with all the other cheap no-name dolls, whose unbendable limbs never stayed in their sockets. He did not have an Olympic medal, or a bitchin' sailboard, or even a pair of sunglasses and swim trunks. Chuck was the kind of guy who'd wear cutoffs to the pool. I'm surprised he didn't come with a six-pack of beer.

I loved my girls too much to let Chuck anywhere near them. I don't know what happened to him. Probably he shacked up under the bed with the Bionic Woman. Superstar and Ballerina gradually became more eccentric and unstable, rather like the Edies of Grey Gardens. They lay around disheveled and half naked most of day, destroyed by the unfulfilled promise of their beauty. Their prince had never come.

As for me, I found a life-size Ken doll to date in my teens, and found revenge in my father's expression every time he saw us together.

"Your mother is very upset about this," he said gruffly, when word reached him that I was seeing "Ken," a twenty-five-year-old part-time model and ski bum who was nearly ten years older than I. Whenever a conversation with one of his daughters stirred up uncomfortable feelings, my father would stiffen and summon "your mother" to speak through him, like he was channeling Ramtha, the 35,000-year-old man. I tried to look concerned. I doubted my mother had caught wind of it, having moved away to study law, taking my preteen sister to live with her. I had insisted with typical, pain-in-the-ass, teenage defiance that I wasn't going anywhere and was, to my astonishment, allowed to stay. I was boarded with a family who my mother mistakenly hoped would act as surrogates, and our house was rented out, since Dad was supposed to go abroad on sabbatical. He drifted instead between friends, relatives, and hotel bars, from which he presided over the occasional father-daughter conference. I came and went from my landlady's house as I pleased, hanging out in bars, skipping class, and sleeping at my boyfriend's place. I was not quite seventeen, but as far as I could see, I was on my own. It was a little late, I thought, sitting across a table from my father in the plush mauve lounge of the Holiday Inn, to be laying down the law.

It's one thing to not get what you want from your parents. That's the grist of anecdote and of character. To not get what you need, that's another matter, less readily transformed from its raw state. Through the mirrored lens of teenage cool, I could see my father was drowning, unable to save himself, let alone take care of anyone else. I could see that pursuing her career was probably my mother's best, last chance at pulling away from the whirlpool that had begun to swirl around him; that there was no time to lose by fighting me or waiting a few more years. In my mind, I saw all that, and I understood. But in my heart, my parents had left me. And there was no magical misfit to pin it on, or turn it into a funny story.

"Is that your dad?" a playmate asked me once, regarding a huge painted portrait of my father that hung above our living room sofa, a flurry of thick black brushstrokes for his long hair and wild beard, his fierce brow.

"Yes," I replied. Her eyes widened.

"Aren't you scared of him?"

Sometimes, yes.

"Of course not," I said.

His poems were in our readers at school, his books, in the library. Teachers and classmates were always asking me, What's it like having a poet for a father?

I never knew how to answer that question. How should I know what it's like? What's it like having your father for a father?

It was wonderful. It was terrible. It was all I ever knew.

He wasn't like other fathers, and ours was not like other families, at least not in my small hometown in the seventies, when the paper mill was still thriving and the little college where he taught English was brand-new.

"Mrs. Collins," I marveled to my third-grade teacher one morning, "when I woke up, there were eighteen people asleep on our living room floor."

My parents had hosted a party the night before, and our living room had been turned into a temporary hostel. At dawn, I tiptoed over the blanketed bodies in my flannel nightgown, counting the fallen like Florence Nightingale on the fields of Crimea.

There may have been eight. It may as well have been eighty, to judge from the elevation of my teacher's eyebrows.

In elementary school, most kids reacted to these glimpses of bohemian home life with curiosity, but in junior high, they branded me a freak. Hardly any of my classmates would have anything to do with me by then. My parents couldn't appreciate how desperate I was to fit in, and my yearning to be ordinary baffled them. They had raised an intelligent, worldly child. I could make a French omelet and recite Shakespeare. I read *Ms.* magazine and *Our Bodies, Ourselves*. I was hip to marketing propaganda. I could understand the concept of peer pressure. So why did I suddenly want to let Jordache advertise on my backside for free? People weren't meant to be used as billboards, they said. You're smarter than that. You're special.

But I didn't want to be smart or special anymore. I wanted to be normal.

I tried to pass with a disguise. Parents, teach your children proper makeup application at home, or they will learn it on the street. My tutor was a petite, busty eighth-grader named Nicki, who was rumored to have Done It, and was a self-proclaimed expert in cosmetology. I was well beneath her social standing, though a grade older, but she couldn't resist such an acute makeover challenge. She came home with me after school one day, her book bag stuffed with beauty products and tools, and went to work. She covered my pimply face with bottled foundation from the drugstore, a noxious-smelling pink suspension of chalk and oil. Over this base, powder blush was applied in dark welts. "Contouring," Nicki explained, making me suck in my cheeks as she colored them the brownish-purple of an old bruise. Thick kohl liner and frosted shadow was applied to my eyes, and my glasses were set aside, though I could barely see without them. My hair was gelled, feathered, curled, and varnished stiff.

I squinted into the mirror, and saw a miracle.

I bounded down the stairs to show my mother. "What do you think?" I asked, eagerly.

My flawlessly complexioned mother, whose own cosmetic bag held a tiny vial of rouge and one pan of blue-green eye shadow from 1966, reacted with equal parts horror and amusement.

"I think you look ridiculous," she blurted.

"You don't know anything!" I shouted, running back up the stairs. Her insistence that I was fine the way I was proved just how little she knew. I was teased for the clothes she liked on me, the embroidered peasant dresses and bib overalls. My classmates sniggered at my unusual name. I wasn't special. I was strange. And I was anything but fine the way I was.

Nicki was still sitting on my bed, peering into a compact. She wore tight blue jeans and an off-shoulder angora sweater. It was said she owned over a dozen of them, and had dated an eighteen-year-old. She glanced up at me through lush curled lashes, surveying her own artisanship with cool satisfaction, then raised one perfectly tweezed eyebrow.

"Never mind," I said, apologetically, tipping my head backward in the direction of the stairs. "I love your sweaters. Where do you buy them?"

Then I shut the door behind me and pushed off, chasing normal.

It's unsettling to me, now, to realize what a dark view I took of being misunderstood by my parents, and how silently I nursed those resentments, both petty and grievous. I'm sure I've already disappointed my own kids more than I know, and they haven't got to middle school yet. We're not even at the *hard* part. The questions I put to my mother about past maternal misdeeds aren't intended to make her feel bad, but to make me feel better. If I can let her off the hook, maybe there's clemency down the road for me.

When the boys were babies, and crying was their only vocabulary for complaints, I longed for them to learn to talk, to tell me exactly what was wrong. But as their language has grown more complex, so have their needs and desires. The list of solutions used to be a short one: there were few problems a snuggle, a snack, or a change of clothes couldn't solve. Once, I had the power to stop bad dreams just by laying my hand on the back of a troubled sleeper. Now the older two can read newspaper headlines about suicide bombers, car crashes, and cancer, nightmares I can't banish, monsters I can't promise aren't real. Longer stretches of their days are spent away from me, of which I only hear selected highlights. They have interactions with friends, teachers, neighbors, and strangers that don't involve me. Just because children can use their words doesn't mean they will. When I consider what proportion of my own childhood lay hidden beneath the surface of my days, the transparency of an earsplitting wail is a relief in a way. At least it's quite obvious that something is the matter.

My middle son, in particular, keeps his cards close to his chest. Quiet and enigmatic by nature, I call him our stealth child. He is extremely sensitive to all input, sensory or otherwise. Sounds are louder, tastes are stronger, smells are smellier, feelings are, well, feelier. Turning inward is his way of taking care of himself in a world that is sometimes too much with him. Prying gets me nowhere, but there's a sweet spot, somewhere between backing off and standing by, where he comes out into the open. Sometimes I meet him there.

A month after starting second grade, he burst through the front door, crying. He and his big brother were tearing across the yard, when he tripped over a tree root and fell, most uncomically, on his funny bone. I ran his arm through a series of highly scientific wiggle tests, and applied an ice pack, but when he was still crying after twenty minutes, and unmoved by his big brother's entreaties every five minutes to "come see this!" I decided a trip to the emergency room was in order. It wasn't like him to stay down for so long. Maybe he had a hairline fracture.

Sitting in the hospital examination room, waiting for an X-ray order, afforded us some rare one-on-one time. I struggled to keep something like a conversation going, never a problem with his chatterbox brothers. I asked him about his arm, and where he was running in such a hurry, and how school was going. We had been in our new neighborhood all summer, long enough for him to make friends with kids in his grade, but I knew it was taking him a little while to find his place.

His answers were typically brief and noncommittal. He was bending and flexing his arm freely, but I still read pain on his face.

"Honey, you look so sad," I said finally. "*Are* you sad?"

He shrugged. "Not really, I guess."

Just like the kids have learned that Mommy's "maybe" means "probably," and Daddy's "maybe" means "unlikely," I have learned that my son's "I guess" means "*you* guess."

"Are your feelings hurt about something?"

"No."

"Are you missing something or somebody?"

"I guess."

It didn't take a full round of twenty questions to find out that he was grieving for his best buddy from his old school. My guy cried quietly into a tissue as I stroked his hair and tried to tell him what I know about friendship and life changes, which is that sometimes it's really hard, and you cry. The elbow was completely healed. I was never so grateful to have wasted an hour on a Sunday afternoon in the ER. Who knows how long my child would have held that grief inside?

Me, me. I do.

A very long time.

I put my arm around him while he wept. I promised we'd call his buddy when we got home, and that I not only understood his feeling sad, I wouldn't be one bit surprised if he felt mad at us for making him change schools.

I felt him uncurl. He twisted a damp piece of tissue in his hands.

"Better?" I said.

"Yeah, but there's just one more thing."

When a child like my child is about to give you something of himself, of his own accord, you sit very still and you breathe very carefully.

"What, honey?"

"I wanted to buy the house we looked at that had the creek in the backyard." I had to think a minute before I could clearly picture it, one of the dozen or so properties we'd looked at in a whirlwind couple of days, over six months before.

The things we hold on to, the length we hold on. His mother's child for sure.

"Trust me," I said, on the day we made the offer on a different house. "Aw," he said quietly, his disappointment barely registering above radar. I was surprised by it, but not deterred. Spring runoff aside, that listing was all wrong for us: bad traffic, a failing school zone, wall-to-wall carpet. It was never a serious contender. I knew he'd forget all about it as soon as we got settled at our new address, a secluded suburban valley teeming with kids, a short bike ride away from a great school and a real creek. I did.

Trust me is what parents tell children when the needle goes in, when the classroom door shuts, when the wish is denied. Don't be afraid, don't worry, don't cry. Someday you'll understand. You'll see.

"Trust me," my father said, standing at the foot of the crumbling stucco stairs where I bolted on our first night in Tobago, upon seeing the concrete box that was to be our home for the next several months while he wrote a play. Lizards clung to the mildewed ceiling and walls. It felt like a cave inside. Outside, it was too dark to see anything but the white wash of stars across the black sky. Spilled milk.

"Trust me," he said, leading me back inside and tucking me in bed. When morning came, I got up quietly, tiptoed past my sleeping family, pushed the louvered door open, and stepped out into a paradise. I was ten years old, and I was living on Robinson Crusoe's island. Who cared what it looked like indoors?

"Trust me," he said, the last time I saw him alive, when I begged him to go to the hospital, because he was dying in a dank cave of an apartment, and there were no stars in that darkness, no hope of seeing things differently in the morning, only the pain and squalor and madness of late-stage alcoholism laid bare. It wasn't going to be all right. The monster was real.

"Trust me," he said, as it devoured him. Don't be afraid, don't worry, don't cry.

Daddy.

"I'm scared," my five-year-old says, not wanting to sleep alone.

"What are you scared of?"

"That something will get me, and you won't know."

I'm scared of that, too.

"Not going to happen," I say. "Trust me."

The words are a prayer, not a warranty. I understand that now.

In the end, the tooth fairy finally comes through, something under the Christmas tree always makes up for what isn't there, and the Easter bunny gets away with all kinds of twitchy behavior as long as he leaves chocolate. Maybe for the kids, these are early exercises in doubt and faith. Or maybe the practice is for me, a way to wean myself slowly from the fond and fierce delusion that it's within my power and duty to see into their hearts, grant all their wishes, and prevent them from ever being hurt or disappointed in life.

The power that comes with being a parent is both awesome and minute. We get to be vanquishers of nightmares, granters of wishes, and readers of minds, with eyes in the back of our heads, and kisses that heal. We are also poor gods, petty dictators, and bad Santas. We are helpless to keep the world, or even ourselves, from ever inflicting pain on our children. Love isn't enough. Instinct isn't enough. Our good intentions aren't nearly enough. The best we can hope for is that it all counts for something, when the jig is up, when someday comes around, when our children finally do understand, and see.

# 11.

# Southern Man

Hell, I got my faults. I admit it.
But hell, I got my ways, too.

—Henry Moon, in the movie *Goin' South*

My oldest son came to me one weekend afternoon, anxious, because he had a Cub Scout woodworking project for which he needed his dad's tools and assistance, and his father did not share his sense of urgency about getting started. The best way to get help from somebody, I explained, is to clearly state what you need, and to ask them nicely. Then I set a trap. I went to Patrick and casually mentioned that Cub Master Chip had invited all the Scouts and parents to come use the power tools in *his* workshop, the implication being that Cub Master Chip's workshop, power tools, and genitals were infinitely superior to anything we had at home. It worked.

"Cub Master Chip is a pussy," my husband declared, marching to the garage to fetch his saw and ordering our son to bring his building materials. A few minutes later, I heard the buzz of a saw outside and felt a surge of satisfaction and pride at the thought of my man teaching our son in the ways of tools and their safe usage. Of course, I had to ruin it by taking a look.

Patrick sat cross-legged on the porch, the vibrating handle of a small power saw positioned vertically in front of his groin, the reciprocating blade parallel to his midriff, the tip pointing straight to his Adam's apple. With one bare hand, he was feeding a block of pinewood to the rapidly moving saw teeth. There were so many major organs and arteries in play I was stunned speechless for a second. A cloud of fine sawdust surrounded him and our three enraptured children.

"Boys, get back!" I shrieked, moving in to shield them. "Oh my God, the banister!"

My husband turned off the saw and rubbed his eyes. "What?" he asked, coughing and blinking.

I hardly knew where to begin. I pointed to a fresh gouge in the porch rail that suggested he had tried traditional methods before rejecting them, using the rail for a sawhorse. "Do you have to do this out here?" I said.

Patrick looked annoyed and bewildered by my objection. "Well," he said, licking his thumb and rubbing the gash in the rail with it, "where else would I do it?"

"The garage? Don't you have some kind of workbench with a clamp or something? And shouldn't you be wearing safety goggles?" I was trying not to be inflammatory, but I couldn't help adding, "The Cub master probably has a workbench."

"Oh yeah, I'll just bet he does," scoffed Patrick. He turned the power back on and returned to aerial freestyle jigsawing. The boys resumed watching and coughing in the dust. I had over-played my hand. Safety goggles and workbenches, indeed.

I made the kids move to a safe distance at the far end of the porch before I retreated indoors, defeated. You can get a southern man to start something, but you can't make him stop.

I should know. They're a lifelong fascination of mine, for which I blame Martin Scorsese and my father. I was eight years old when Dad took me to me to see Scorsese's 1978 rock docu-mentary, *The Last Waltz*. We took our seats in a near-empty the-ater and waited for the movie to start. I glanced back and forth between my father's profile, and the dark and silent screen he was fixed upon so intensely, wondering what was about to hap-pen. There was a flash like lightning, then the opening guitar lick, and the entire frame exploded into light and sound. It was like the birth of a new solar system, with drummer Levon Helm the burning sun at its center. He was wailing about the Missssissippi-rivah, eyes shut, face incandescent. He was a portrait of ecstatic abandon, thrilling to watch and to hear. I had barely caught my breath after his last yodel, when a crazy-looking wild man strut-ted onstage, a confederate eagle swooping down the crown of his white straw hat. "The Hawk," Daddy breathed, reverently, and Ronnie Hawkins howled ravenously, "Who do you love?" I gripped the armrests and pushed my spine into the velvet seat back as far as it could go. It was the Hawk, Daddy explained in a whisper, who led Levon Helm out of Arkansas to Canada, where they started The Band, whose legendary last concert we were watching. It was a tidy bit of foreshadowing, since I would grow up and trace the same migratory path in reverse. But that future was still a speck, drifting unnoticed across the projector beam.

Nothing beyond the big screen existed for me in that moment. Ronnie Hawkins was as terrifying as Levon Helm was mesmerizing, but there was something about both of them that made every other star on the stage seem dimmer. There was *something* about southern men. The hook was set.

"Mesmerized and terrified" pretty much sums up the experience of falling in love with my southern-born-and-bred husband, nearly twenty years later. The first time I spoke to my new e-mail pal on the telephone, I thought maybe he was having me on. I had never heard anyone speak like that outside of television and the movies. I was enchanted by his soft drawl, the way he could draw out a one-syllable word into two or three, and the hint of country twang in his inflections—considerably toned down, as I gleaned later from hearing him talk to his family and childhood friends. When he got bold enough to call me "sugar," ice crystals in my northern blood melted and sizzled.

When he sent me a picture in the mail, I surveyed it as if it was a topographical map, and decided his was a face that could only have come from the South. He had long blond hair, sleepy green eyes, and deep lines around his mouth. His craggy features were boyish and ancient at the same time, and made me think of moonshine stills and blood feuds. Something in his eyes hinted at acts of defiance and reckless valor. Only my romantic daydreams didn't anticipate how often it would be me who was being defied, like the time he flew 2,500 miles to see me on the spur of the moment, over my sputtered objections.

"Fortune favors the bold," he proclaimed, as I sat on the edge of his hotel bed to tell him he shouldn't have come, that his was a hopeless gamble. Thinking he should at least eat something before I sent him back to Arkansas forever, I brought him a bucket of southern fried chicken, from an American franchise that had opened next to one of the dozen or so excellent fish-and-chip shops in my East Coast town. As if he were a koala bear and could eat only food from his native habitat.

"I love you," I told him, as he sniffed the chicken skeptically and set it aside. "But I can't be with you." I didn't know how to say that being near him made me want to throw up, not from revulsion, but from the force of my own heightened emotions. I had panic attacks when we were together, and I felt like I might die when we were apart. I didn't know whether I was in love or having an emergency.

He went back that time, but he never gave up. Like I said, you can start something with a southern man, but you can't make him stop.

By the time I met Patrick, I'd forgotten that Levon Helm came from Arkansas. Everybody in the world mocks Americans for being ignorant of geography beyond their own border, but all I knew about the twenty-fifth state was that the new American president came from there. Before Bill Clinton, I didn't even know how to pronounce Arkansas. I thought it was pronounced Ar-KAN-zuss, and was adjunct to Kansas. Like North and South Dakota, or the Carolinas. Kansas and Ar-Kansas. If I had to come up with a mental image, it would have been borrowed straight from *The Wizard of Oz* or *The Grapes of Wrath*: tumbleweeds and twisters. I didn't realize that it was part of the mythic American South (though the Old South scarcely recognizes it as such, situated as it is in the wilderness west of the Mississippi). But Arkansas is planted deep in Dixie, with cotton fields and magnolia trees, antebellum mansions and sharecropping shacks, blues music and barbecue pits. Among its less charming bona fides are slavery, Jim Crow, rednecks, and wrathful religion.

It was springtime when I arrived, after spending the winter with Patrick in Mexico. "Well, what do you think?" he asked, sitting beside me in Lucy, his '64 Comet, on the interstate between Texarkana and Little Rock. That car drove like a manta ray swims, undulating from side to side as it glided over the asphalt. The warm vinyl stuck to my bare legs. Empty cigarette packages and ashes were scattered around our feet. Our money was all gone, our bridges all burned. Now what?

I looked out the side window and shrugged indifferently. Dense stands of trees lined the highway. I hadn't expected it to be so green. "Bushy," I replied.

I didn't know what to call things, the vocabulary of the land. I knew the pine, but not the hickory or the sweet gum. There was no spruce or birch, no alders. I didn't have the words to see: black oak, buckeye, dogwood. I saw forest, not trees. It was claustrophobic. Having lived on an island for most of my life, I was used to being able to gaze into the distance. The spacious high desert felt more like home to me. Here, even in April, the foliage was so lush it writhed. The vines that covered the trees seemed to be reaching out, conspiring to tie me down.

I resisted at first. I didn't care to learn the names of things. I liked being a stranger, which was fortunate, since the mentality, if not the geography, of the South *is* an island. I was what we in Newfoundland call a "come-from-away," an outsider. I knew it was useless to try to blend in, so I made the most of my strangeness, enjoying the license it afforded me. For the first few years, I had a kind of diplomatic immunity when it came to transgressing the cryptic and convoluted code of southern behavior, aka "act right." I was generally forgiven for not knowing any better, a benefit of the doubt that southerners don't extend to their fellow citizens who come from the North. I was a foreigner, but at least I was no Yankee.

Let's locate this South before I make another sweeping generalization about its sons and daughters. There are seventeen states that the U.S. Census Bureau calls the South. There are eleven states of the Old Confederacy that history designates as the South. But those definitions are just flimsy overlays on a map. The real South exists in the collective imagination of those who call themselves southerners; it's a compilation of stories that happen to be set in a particular place, often having very little to do with actual history, culture, or individuals. But that's neither here nor there. Just because a story isn't factual doesn't mean it isn't true.

One of these stories is that southerners are the trustees of higher civilization and social graces. Obviously, there are ignorant and boorish people everywhere, and plenty of the worst examples say "y'all," fluently. Neither does genteel refinement make someone courteous or kind. There's a self-congratulatory aspect of "act right" that can be downright ugly when it's flung around in contempt. You can coat that shit in sugar, but it's still shit. Still, there is a value on decorum here that transcends class divisions and very often finds sincere and gracious expression. It's almost archaic, and it took some getting used to. I found it oddly formal at first that children were expected to answer their own parents with "No, ma'am" and "Yes, sir," and quaint that they put "Miss" or "Mister" in front of adult family friends' first names. It took me a while to become attuned to the roundabout way southerners have of communicating. Sometimes it was all I could do to keep from asking someone to get to their ever-loving point, if they even had one. I still haven't figured out why it is preferable to stand behind someone in the grocery aisle, seething resentment, rather than come out and politely ask if they might move their cart aside, but I do know what it means when the subject is deftly changed mid-conversation (they disagree strongly with something you said), and that "Bless her heart" translates to "That is one crazy bitch." I cannot imagine speaking English anymore without the indispensable pronoun "y'all," equivalent to the French *vous*, in that it provides an oblique way of addressing someone, instead of the more intrusive and intimate "you."

By the time "y'all" crept into my vernacular, I was acculturated, and my diplomatic pass was revoked. I can't claim anymore not to know better. I am expected to act right, and I have come to expect it of others, though we all fail regularly. I've lived in the South long enough to absorb the story, and perpetuate it. I find it jarring now to travel to parts of the country where people don't hold doors for one another, or are blunt-spoken and abrupt with strangers. It's possible, on such occasions, I have glanced down my nose at a very slight angle, and thought, *Yankees.*

Like the Old Testament, the stories of the South don't always line up. Southerners have strong, and often contradictory, opinions about what is, or isn't, bona fide. I'm not one to let ignorance keep me on the sidelines of a good argument. I read *Southern Living*. I've seen *Gone With the Wind*. And I've drunk quite a lot of bourbon in my time. I think those credentials are unimpeachable, but my husband resists my attempts to correct him on the finer points of southern culture, particularly when it comes to food. Take, for example, strawberry shortcake. I prefer a biscuit-style shortcake, which Patrick refers to as "some northern idea of shortcake." I insist it is true southern shortcake, one, holy, and apostolic. The oily sponge-cake-based abomination he thinks of as shortcake, I tell him, is not a *southern* delicacy at all, but a trailer park one. It's the trailer trash card, and I am not above playing it to win the culture war at home.

I ought to be ashamed. Patrick was raised in trailer parks, but there was nothing trashy about his upbringing. Like plenty of folks whose homes are factory made, as I was to discover when I moved here, his parents were respectable and fastidious people, who worked hard and lived modestly. They weren't sophisticates, but they didn't match up with the stereotype either. His dad was a meter man for the light company, and his mom, an office clerk. They put two sons through braces, cars, and college; helping them with mortgage down payments and seeing them through tight spots. Their homes may have been mobile, but that family was built on a rock-solid foundation. I never knew anything like it, though the house I grew up in had a poured basement and my parents had college degrees. But I have no scruples when it comes to being right. I have played the trailer trash card over scratch biscuits versus canned, cornbread with sugar versus cornbread without, sweetened iced tea versus unsweetened, mustard-based barbecue sauce over molasses-based, drop dumplings versus rolled, cheese grits versus plain.

Patrick is impervious to my siege. He's not insecure about his upbringing or his preferences. The closest he ever comes to conceding are the times he will allow with a snort that perhaps biscuit-style shortcake is what they eat back east on the coast or in some other pretentious, carpetbag-infiltrated part of the South, but it doesn't have a place in his South. "That's just some shit you read in a book," he'll say, and he almost always has me there.

Food is gospel in the South. Nothing, not even guns, is considered as sacred. Cooking and eating are the highest form of storytelling there is. Recipes serve as heirlooms and pedigrees, to be passed from generation to generation. When I married Patrick, I inherited a wealth of them, but the jewel in the family crown is cornbread dressing.

The savory bread mixture that northerners stuff into birds before roasting is considered by southerners to be an abomination in the sight of the Lord. Cornbread dressing, baked in a separate pan, is what is served with Thanksgiving turkey, and every family has its own recipe. Ours came down Patrick's maternal line, and was thought to be unique until I learned that a friend in North Carolina inherited a very similar recipe, proving she and my husband are related by dressing. If DNA mutations can track human migration patterns, why not culinary adaptations? We may never know when or why my sons' Scots-Irish ancestors started pushing westward from the Carolinas through Georgia, Alabama, and on to Arkansas. But it looks as if somewhere along the way they added eggs to the cornbread dressing. Call it manifest destiny.

I used to make the dressing myself, but in recent years, Patrick has taken over, appointing our eldest son as his apprentice. My in-laws died within a few years of each other. Their last mobile home—a prefab on a beautifully landscaped country lot—was sold, and the extended family drifted into diaspora. Unless you count photographs and a couple of pieces of furniture, there's nothing tangible to connect our children to their Arkansas grandparents. Until we make dressing.

My contribution is to bake up cornbread in the cast-iron skillet I chose as a memento from my mother-in-law's kitchen after she died. A well-seasoned skillet is a treasure, something no southern kitchen can be without. Mothers traditionally pass them on to daughters. I am meticulous in protecting that skillet, as I am about very few objects, never letting a drop of soap near the gleaming black surface. I think Millie would be proud to know I have it, and would say I've earned it, even if I am a foreigner. I knew her only a short time, but I loved her, as she was beloved by all her family and friends. To the grandchildren who knew her, she was "Honey," engraved upon her headstone beneath her name.

On Thanksgiving eve, I listen to her son reading aloud to his son the steps written in his mother's lovely hand. Amid the egg cracking and the cornbread crumbling, he tells stories about Thanksgivings past, and explains the difference between cornbread dressing and bread stuffing. True religion.

"You were born in the South, son. Don't ever forget that." He says it loud enough to be sure I can hear, and when I look up, I can see the teasing gleam in his eyes, daring me to make something of it.

When we're not talking about food and good manners, I have conflicted feelings about the place of southern pride in my sons' psyches. It's a sensitive topic, because you can't separate southern pride from southern shame. It's not possible to invoke a glorious South without calling up the ignominious one. Slavery and segregation are entwined at its roots. My children don't have to dig very deep to find racism. Patrick warned me, when I came to Arkansas, that his parents were "old-fashioned," but I never got used to the shock of hearing racial slurs coming from the mouths of people whom I knew to be so kind and loving in every other regard. To hear them casually drop the N-word or tell a racist joke was always blindsiding. I wanted to believe that the words were simply the hollow remnants of a bygone age; that they came from ignorance and obstinacy, not hatred. My in-laws grew up in a society where such language and thinking were not just acceptable, they were institutional. Patrick's mother's senior high school class was disrupted by the landmark desegregation crisis that shut down Little Rock Central High in the fifties. I had seen images of the mob all my life; the white teenagers and adults with their faces twisted in rage, the terrified black students clutching their schoolbooks. I was raised by liberal intellectuals, in a place that had virtually no racial minority population. From that high, academic vantage point, it was easy to look down on racism and racists, and condemn both as pure and simple evil. Encountering it in real people didn't convince me that racism was any less wrong, but it did teach me that it's quite a bit more complicated.

I was disturbed by some of the accepted conventions I encountered, and curious about a whole lot of others. Why did so many white southerners say "He's black" sotto voce when describing someone? Was it a *secret* that the person was black? Was it rude to observe that they were? And why was it that when white girls got drunk, they almost always started talking to each other like inner-city black girls? Did it go both ways, I wondered. When black girls partied, did they think it was fun to talk like white sorority girls?

But you weren't supposed to ask those kinds of questions. I went to a poetry reading with an African-American friend where I was the only white person. I wasn't uncomfortable, but it seemed strange to me. Did it seem strange to him, I wanted to know, so I asked. Not cool, said Patrick, when I told him. You're not supposed to notice.

But how could you not? The roar of all that went unseen, unsaid, and unasked was deafening, like white noise.

The worst thing is, after a while, you stop hearing it.

*

"Why do they call it the Hood?" my mother asked innocently, gazing through the passenger-side window at the dilapidated homes that surrounded Little Rock Central High. She thought it was the official name of the district, like SoHo or the Haight, a proper noun you'd see emblazoned on banners attached to lampposts. Welcome to the Historic Hood District!

I thanked God I had vetoed her idea to walk, not that I would have let my mom, fresh off the plane from Canada, walk to Central High. I could just see her asking a crack addict for directions to the Hood. I explained that it was slang for "neighborhood," and that it was synonymous with "ghetto." As we drove past boarded-up doors and broken windows, I told her about white flight, how after the school was integrated, there had been an exodus of white families to the suburbs and a boom in private schools. I told her about the gangs, crack houses, and drive-bys.

My mother's face was crestfallen. Visiting Central High was a pilgrimage for her. I might as well have told her the moon landing had been faked, and the Vietnam War was still going on.

"What was it all for, then?" she asked. "What's changed?"

"I don't know," I said, turning back onto the freeway that slices this city in two, cutting the black urban neighborhoods off, like a necrotic limb, from the affluent white ones. Its construction began shortly after desegregation. "I don't know."

When I was nine years old, I flew with my family to Trinidad. It was my first time in the tropics, and I'll never forget how it felt to step out of the plane, into equatorial air so choked with humidity that it was viscous. When I first came to the South, the issue of race felt like that to me; pervasive and displacing. But people who lived and breathed it all their lives seemed acclimatized to it, whether they were black or white. Eventually I was, too. I can't pretend to be above it anymore. I'm immersed, saturated. Racism is embedded in the news media, in our institutions, and in the infrastructure of our communities. My sons are heirs to it. On parents' day at my youngest child's private preschool, he announced an ambition to grow up to be a garbageman, and all of us white parents smiled and said that it was a fine thing to be, and felt safe doing so, because *of course* none of our children will grow up to be a garbageman. Every garbageman they've ever seen is black.

Of course I'm well aware that systemic racism is a problem for all of America, not just the South. In fact, I think it's *the* problem for America. White southerners often feel like they are the scapegoat for the sins of a whole nation, and they've got a valid point. But it's been only half a century since doorways and drinking fountains here were labeled "white" or "colored," not long enough to call it history. Though the signs have come down, segregation persists, in reality if not in policy. For ten years, we lived in a neighborhood that most consider to be the epicenter of liberalism in Little Rock, the kind with bumper stickers in every driveway: yes to a woman's choice and the environment, no to war and gated communities. And yet that neighborhood is the whitest place I've ever lived, even more than the town I grew up in, if that's possible. There are gates, and then there are gates. At least the ones with guardhouses and no trespassing signs are being honest about it.

I know there are enclaves like our old neighborhood in every city in America, and I sympathize with those who bristle at the suggestion that the South is stuck in its racist past. But it's not just northerners, or African-Americans, who can't let it go. I'm not sure where else in the world you could live and routinely encounter men in uniforms from a war that supposedly ended nearly 150 years ago. A Civil War reenactor was the surprise highlight at last year's Cub Scout banquet, and it was a good thing there was no question-and-answer period, because I had some pointed ones regarding period costume for slaves of the Confederate States of America.

The Civil War is a part of my sons' heritage I've struggled with for a long time. Family legend has it that they are related to a celebrated martyr of the Confederacy, David O. Dodd, a seventeen-year-old message boy whose trial and execution are reenacted in Little Rock every year. It's interesting, and I don't want them to feel ashamed of it, but is it something I want them to feel proud of? I had no answer for that question until we went to Gettysburg last summer, a side excursion on an epic road trip north. One hundred and forty-six years to the day that the first shots were fired, I watched my sons play in the shadow of an enormous oak that must have grown out of the earth while it was still bloody.

"Come over here," I called to them softly, after absorbing the figures and dates on the interpretive marker. I swept my arm out in front of me, and described to them what I saw in my mind's eye: men and boys, some not much older than my ten-year-old, marching onto the field. It had taken us three days to drive from Arkansas, I reminded them. Imagine if you had to walk. How tired and ragged they must have been. How determined.

I turned to my boys, so full of passion and persistence, the two traits I value above all others but kindness. They come by it honestly. They are their father's sons. Sons of the South.

"People say they were fighting for lots of reasons, but they were defending people who kept other people as slaves. It was wrong, and it was a good thing they lost."

I let that sink in, before adding, "The Confederates weren't all bad people. And the Union soldiers weren't all good." I wondered what it was like to be a mother of young children on the path of Sherman's March.

"People do terrible things to each other in wars," I told them, ending the lesson, and letting them get back to climbing on the cannons. I strolled a few paces over to Patrick, hoping he wasn't baiting any of the other visitors with talk of the "War of Northern Aggression."

"I had a talk with the boys about the war," I reported.

"What did you tell them?"

"That the North had the just cause, but they were douchebags."

He laughed. "That sounds about right."

We loaded the kids in the van, and drove off slowly toward another field.

"Arkansas!" the boys shouted as we came upon a granite memorial.

We pulled over and got out to read the inscription, the usual stuff about blood, valor, and hallowed ground.

"Such a fucked-up, stupid thing," I heard my husband say, in a low, thick voice. I looked over, and saw with surprise that there were tears on his cheeks. It amazes me how deep are the wounds of that war. It makes ghosts of the living, compels them to reenact that mistake, over and over, so no one can move on. Southern men. Always starting something they can't stop.

I looked back at the monument to the fallen, thinking that the words Patrick just spoke made a better epitaph for them. Fortune doesn't always favor the bold.

"That sounds about right," I told him. "Let's move on."

# 12

# A Pilgrim's Progress

Across America, the onset of winter is heralded by a spectacular show of fall color that begins in late October and peaks toward the end of November. This riotous display spills forth from our mailboxes and newspapers, in the form of glossy sales flyers reminding us that Thanksgiving is coming, and that it's going to take a lot of new stuff to make us properly thankful this year. We'll need a moving truck of new furniture and appliances, tableware to seat fifty, guest linens and inflatable mattresses to sleep twenty, matching cashmere turtlenecks for the whole family, and—this was in the warehouse club holiday flyer a few years ago—a small jet. Because a good hostess is always prepared.

It's hard not to get swept up in it. There is rarely anyone but me, my husband, and our kids around our Thanksgiving table, but that doesn't keep me from fretting over my mismatched dishes and tragic lack of a guest suite, as I thumb through the flyers and spin a daydream in which I usher a steady stream of guests toward monogrammed hand towels and ingenious place cards. Financial reality delivers me from most temptation, but I am vulnerable in Target, where the dream—or snippets of it— appears to hover more nearly within reach. It's a dangerous illusion, because shopping at Target is like sawing down the leg of a table. You get one cute, hip thing for your house, and it makes all the things that aren't cute and hip stand out. One of my friends calls it the "hundred-dollar-an-hour store." I find this formula to be uncannily accurate, and if she actually came up with the algebra on her own, she ought to be chairing the Federal Reserve.

I'll walk in there with a list that reads "Batteries, Velcro," and walk out ninety minutes later with a receipt for $144. In between coming and going is the spiral descent into the heart of darkness, the vortex of the red bull's-eye. The unraveling is accompanied by an internal dramatic monologue that swells to operatic heights, an aria from a beggar's opera:

It starts in the key of innocent wistfulness.

*O, what pretty dishes! I wish I had pretty dishes!*

Then, the rationalization begins, *andante*.

*Someone might stop by for dinner, or dessert. We'll need more dishes. These are practical. And on clearance.*

Now, the bargaining, *allegro*.

*I won't buy the hand towels I saw on sale two aisles back. I'll cut our budget back somewhere else. I will positively, absolutely, not go overboard with the holiday menu, and I'll just forget I ever saw that table lamp over there.*

The drama builds, with hostility and wheedling, *cadenza*.

*For God's sake, they're just five dollars a plate. Is it so terrible to want to splurge a little? You think so-and-so would think twice about spending a few dollars on* her *Thanksgiving table? CAN'T I EVER HAVE ANYTHING NICE FOR ONCE IN MY LIFE?*

To the checkout, fait accompli, *pianissimo.* The fat lady has sung. *Grazie.*

The irony is that Thanksgiving Day itself is singularly uncommercial. There are no gifts or cards to be purchased and exchanged. The focus is simply and sincerely on appreciating what you already have. It is the one pause in the otherwise relentless carousel of consumerism in this country, and we can barely keep it up for twenty-four hours. The release of all that pent-up energy the next morning is awesome to behold—from a safe distance. It's like the running of the bulls in Spain. Black Friday should be written up in international travel magazines as an American ritual not to be missed.

All of it was utterly foreign to me when I first came here. I grew up observing something that Canadians call Thanksgiving, but there it is a minor holiday, celebrated in October, with a meal on the scale of a nice Sunday dinner. There are no pilgrims or cornucopias, no particular history or sentiment attached to the occasion. As far as I can tell, it was co-opted for the sake of a long weekend. I had no idea how much was lost in the translation until I pulled up a chair and sat down to the real thing. My first thought was that it was an insane amount of food. I'd had six months of American supersizing by that time, but I was still staggered at the bounty and variety of dishes involved. The turkey, gravy, and pumpkin pie were familiar, but I was out of my depth after that. In addition to pumpkin, there were apple, chocolate, pecan, and various cream pies. There were multiple pans of corn-bread dressing, rolls, and biscuits. There were strange fifties-style casseroles: sweet potatoes topped with marshmallows, and green beans swimming in canned mushroom soup. It was all delicious, but it seemed excessive, and redundant. Why the big feast and get-together, only to have to pull off a reprise a mere month later, at Christmas? I didn't get it. I shook my head and tsk-tsked at the *typical* lack of restraint.

It was years before I stopped thinking *You're doing it wrong,* and realized that Thanksgiving isn't a spoiler to the American winter holiday season, but the actual kickoff. As soon as the last turkey leftover is wrapped, the reindeer games are on. The mental adjustment helped me feel less out of sync with the season, but I still lagged. I no longer derided my neighbors for putting their Christmas trees up right after Thanksgiving, but I couldn't bring myself to trim ours before mid-December. As it's taking your chances to score a real tree after mid-December, my cultural noncompliance introduced a note of suspense to what otherwise might have been a blandly predictable holiday season for the children. It *had* to be a real tree. Anytime I reached out to finger the lifelike tip of an artificial, prelit display model, I heard my father's voice in my head, barking, "Fake tree, fake Christmas!" causing me to jerk my hand back like I had touched fire. I couldn't turn my back on tradition. Christmas wouldn't be Christmas without someone swearing over missing rope, burned-out lights, and tee-tering tree stands. Far be it from me to break the chain.

For a while, we bridged the culture gap by driving to a local tree farm on Thanksgiving weekend, tagging a tree and paying for it, then leaving it in the ground until we came back for it, three weeks later. That added up to a whole lot of driving around, and every year I gained a little more appreciation for trees whose synthetic branches would never touch a roof rack. The whole excursion felt contrived, anyway. It wasn't as if we were trekking through the hushed, snowy woods, Daddy's axe in hand, like we did when I was a little girl. We were at a U-Pick in the middle of a sodden field, with country music blaring over the PA system. Finally, one December when I was in the throes of a deadline, with no long afternoons to spare for a country drive, I broke down (in Target, naturally) and bought an enormous fake tree. I brought it home and popped it open like a beach umbrella. And do you know what, boys and girls? Christmas CAME. It came without puddles. It came without tipping. Without shedding needles, or sticky sap dripping. It came without rope, or getting stuck in the door.

"Maybe Christmas," I thought, "*does* come from a store."

There was no going back, once I'd seen the prelit light. I love everything about our fake Christmas tree, even the jolt of panic when I realize I forgot all day to water it, followed by the realization that I *didn't* forget. Gets me every time. It's a little adrenaline high.

The kids are somewhat reassured to know that our tree is secured and on standby in the attic, but they still get a little anxious when all the halls in the world but ours seem decked and trimmed. I remember worrying that Christmas preparations in my childhood home weren't quite up to code either. I was gravely concerned that our house had no fireplace. Even after my parents explained that Santa could just as easily use the front door, I wasn't entirely convinced there wouldn't be some sort of penalty imposed; items crossed from my list. I knew it was not the done thing to hang your stocking over a nail in the plywood stereo stand.

There are a few compensating charms to raising a family on this little raft of ours, stranded as we are from in-laws, grandparents, cousins, and the like. Getting to make up our own traditions is one of them. Who's to tell us, "That's not how we do it"? To tide the kids over, we introduced the Saint Nicholas tree, a cheap tabletop tree that lives in the attic and comes out on December 6, the saint's feast day. It's *their* tree, and I keep my mitts off it, no matter how clumped together all the red balls are or how big the hole in the lights is. This is where they get to hang all the ornaments that come from fast-food places, the plastic cartoon characters, the dollar-store nativity figurines with their pasty bisque complexions. It's where kitsch comes to nest.

Adopting Saint Nicholas Day was supposed to provide a soft landing for when the kids eventually let go of Santa—giving them a historical figure for a transitional object. The first time we set up their little tree, I explained that it honored the memory of a Turkish bishop who lived—and died—a long time ago. He wasn't supposed to be magical. But when they found gold-wrapped chocolate coins in their shoes the next morning, they assumed they came from Saint Nicholas, and were so excited by the idea, I had to go along with it. My kids make a believer out of me.

It's amazing how many holes in a story can be spackled over with a little willingness to believe. When I was nine years old, my next-door neighbor told me point-blank that she'd seen my parents buying one of my Christmas presents at Kmart. I barely flinched. She might as well have told me that it wasn't really our dolls talking when we played with them. So it was make-believe. That didn't mean it wasn't *real*. I understood then that my parents were in a game of pretend with me—a really good game. Why would I spoil our fun by not playing along?

Then I grew up, and forgot how to play. I grappled over the Santa question with all the earnestness a new parent can muster. Would we be perpetuating a hoax? Was it a betrayal of trust? How would we explain everything? And just how far was I willing to run with it? I established complex ethical guidelines to minimize our liability. We'd keep the story simple and vague. We would use the word "Santa" as a euphemism for the spirit of giving. We would neither confirm nor deny reports that Santa Claus is, or is not, a real person. That, and all other inquiries, should be volleyed back to the inquirer, so as not to incriminate ourselves. We'd say things like, "How do *you* think he gets around to all those houses in a single night?" The distribution of gifts would not be tied to merit, and above all, we would never, *ever* invoke Santa Claus as a threat.

That lasted until the first child could squeak "Santa!" Spirit, my ass. Would a spirit leave cookie crumbs and half-nibbled carrots all over the coffee table? Does a spirit make hoofprints across the floor? Can you track a spirit on the computer using radar? Do letters from spirits get postmarked from the North Pole? Would NASA lie? Would the U.S. Postal Service? I hope Santa didn't hear you think that, because, oh yeah, he *reads minds*. You better *not* shout.

Threats? Listen, after three kids, you use whatever leverage you can get. As far as mine are concerned, the naughty-or-nice tip line has operators standing by, 24/7.

How far am I willing to run with it?

As far as my boys will take me.

The one bit of Christmas magic I can't work for them,

unfortunately, is snow. Christmas is always green where we live. A couple of times a year, it gets cold enough for the dog's water bowl to freeze over, an event that my children greet with a level of excitement that is completely out of proportion and, frankly, pathetic. A lump of cloudy ice with a couple of hickory leaves stuck in it is hardly a winter wonderland. But it is to them. "Snow!" they shriek if it should happen to sleet or hail, running outside to frolic in the ice pellets.

Real snowfall is a phenomenon we only experience every few years, and when it does happen, is fleeting. When a writing assignment took us all to Quebec last year on a ski vacation, the kids ran around gathering armfuls of snow to their chests in a wild panic. "It's okay, boys," I assured the hoarders. "It will still be here in the morning. I promise."

I like to ski, and it was fun to watch them play, but I don't miss it much myself. Having spent my first twenty-six years in the northeast, I'm thoroughly over winter. The first time it snowed after I moved to Arkansas, I spent the whole day in bed with all the blinds closed, unmoved by my husband's whooping and hollering as he rummaged our drawers for winter clothing.

"Now, where's my toboggan?"

I poked my head out, groundhog style. Our apartment was small. If he had a large wooden sled, I would have noticed it.

"Your what?"

"My toboggan. You know, for my head."

"You mean a *hat*?"

"I mean my toboggan! The wool one. With the puffy thing on top." He batted at an imaginary pom-pom above his head, and I realized he was referring to the kind of knitted hat that Canadians call a "toque." He had his winter vocabulary confused.

"That is *not* a toboggan," I said, with the loud, deliberate pronouncement of a foreign-language tutor. "A toboggan is a waxed plank with a curled end and a rope handle." Someone had to help these people.

"You don't wear a toboggan on your head," I explained to him. "You jump on it with your siblings, point it at a stand of trees, and hurl yourselves downhill at thirty miles an hour screaming, 'LEAN!'"

"Here's my toboggan!" he exclaimed happily, pulling on a toque and racing outside to throw snowballs at the window.

When I did get out the next day, I was astounded by what I saw. It had been a six-inch snowfall, more than sufficient to bring a city without road-clearing equipment to a dead halt for several days. A half-foot of snow hardly qualifies as a dusting where I come from. What amazed me was the sheer economy of use. It seemed like every lawn had a snowman, as if an army of them had invaded and now stood sentinel awaiting further orders.

Since there were no actual toboggans, kids were sliding on anything they could find, cardboard, trash can lids, their own bottoms. A very few had wooden sleds with runners, hauled out of attics for the first time in years. Adults were walking around their front yards with the pomp and deliberation of the first moonwalk. Nobody was wasting one flake of this snow.

The next time we had that kind of snowfall, I had children. I still would have preferred to spend the day in bed with the curtains drawn, but I felt an instinctual obligation to teach my offspring something about winter, lest they perish trying to keep their heads warm with a sled. We bundled up and ventured out into the yard.

"Right," I said, picking up a garden shovel. "First, we pile all the snow into a mound."

As we piled it higher and higher, I sensed that we were being watched. Neighbors were standing at their windows. Passersby were pausing in the street. This was no snowman under construction, obviously. The strange northern woman was *up* to something. They stared as I packed the pile of snow into a compact dome, and then carved out a cave. It's the dugout method of snow fort building. Simple, classic, and architecturally sound.

I dug until my whole body would fit inside. The neighbors probably thought I was getting ready to hibernate. They must have been alarmed when I brought the baby inside with me, but we reemerged before they came running. The children didn't much care for being enveloped in an icy chamber. I thought it was rather homey myself, having spent half my childhood in one. My own mother believed that indoor air was poisonous. "Get some fresh air," she'd say, tossing us kids outside, even on the coldest winter days. Nearly immobilized by our snowsuits, we would trudge around the yard in circles, with my younger sister having to be dug out of a crevice periodically. Eventually, we would dig a shelter out of a snowbank with our mittened hands and huddle there until called for supper.

I feel a twinge of guilt that my own children are deprived of the adventure. Winters—real winters—are fun for children. It's like having a theme park show up in your own backyard every year. And a fresh, deep snowfall really is beautiful. My mother sends us photos of her house at Christmas, with the shrubbery all sugared and drifts of white powder clinging to the recesses of the door. I confess the image stirs up nostalgia; the baptismal quality of new snow, its ability to confer innocence on all the blemished world outside.

But I know too much. Whenever my southern-born-and-bred

husband muses about moving north, I tell him that he really has no idea what he'd be in for.

"Think how much you hate to mow the lawn," I tell him, by way of analogy. "Imagine if you had to mow every single morning, just to get out the driveway. Then, just as you reach the end, someone comes along with a tractor and rolls sod back over it. Oh yeah, and the car doors are frozen shut."

I try to explain to him how long northern winter is, how it drags on and on like a bad marriage, till no one can remember the wonderland that once was. The pristine drifts turn into banks of ice that become decrepit over time, soiled by dog droppings and dirt. They don't melt so much as decay, rotting slowly under the early-spring sunshine.

What I do miss about deep snow, especially at holiday time, is the enforced dormancy, the way it necessarily slows things down. The main drawback I've found in a green Christmas is that there's no excuse to hibernate, no reason why you can't spend every day from Thanksgiving to New Year's Eve shopping, decorating, and baking, which is exactly what the glossy sales flyers encourage us to do. The festivity is relentless. I carve out a little space in it by observing Advent. It's not time yet, I tell the boys, when the manger in the crèche is empty, and they wonder if I have forgotten the baby who belongs in it. I want them to know about waiting, the fullness of time. What it means to lean into not knowing. That's what Advent is about, and it creates an interesting tension, because that's not what the holidays are at all about. I like the quiet introspection that the lengthening darkness affords, but I also hate to miss out on any fun. So I release our merrymaking in increments. Outdoor decorations go up soon after Thanksgiving, and indoor ones a few weeks later. The crèche is populated gradually. The Advent wreath is lit, one candle a week until December 25, after which I cling with orthodox devotion to all twelve days of Christmas, mostly because it gives me a respectable excuse for not getting around to putting the tree away. Just as the kids do with their Saint Nicholas tree, I arrange the season in a way that makes sense to me—never mind what it's supposed to look like. It's become a bit of this and a bit of that, like my Thanksgiving table setting. Like me.

## 13.

# The Facts of Life

On Valentine's Day, my boys came home from school with their doily-trimmed shoe boxes, dumped all the contents out, and immediately began separating candy from the valentines, without so much as a glance at the cards or the messages printed thereon, as if they were candy wrappers, nothing more.

I retrieved the cards, shuffling through them with interest. "Did you get any *special* valentines from anyone?" I asked. They thought I meant one with extra candy.

I tried a different angle. "Did you give a valentine to anyone *special?*"

All three looked at me blankly, cheeks stuffed.

"Like a *girl?*" I asked.

"Like a *wombat?*" I may as well have suggested. They regarded the question as a total non sequitur, glanced at each other with a shrug, and resumed shucking valentines.

I can't tell if their complete indifference to girls is normal or not. I'm not sure how it works with boys, at what age they become interested in romance. I can't remember ever *not* being interested in it. I was four years old the first time I got married, to a neighbor boy I chased—literally—around the yard and dragged before a friend's father who had agreed to officiate. I don't remember what I wore, but I know that I held a potted geranium.

Like many young marriages, ours didn't last. I fell for another man on the first day of kindergarten. Tony was standing alone at the back of the room, crying for his mother. I never could resist a lost boy. I walked over and took his hand in mine, and from that moment, until he moved to Minnesota later that year, we were together. Our families became friends, and we had sleepovers, talking long into the night about sex. Or what we thought sex might be. It had something to do with men and women getting naked, but beyond that, we had no clue. Our conversations were curious but chaste. It didn't occur to either of us to do more than talk about it.

I kept a special place in my heart for Tony, but from first to fifth grade, I was in love with a boy we'll call David O'Neill (since that was his name). David O'Neill was a dreamboat, with dusky olive skin and dark, long-lashed eyes. He was quiet. He was smart. He was nice. I loved him in secret until I was nine years old and in grade four, when my parents separated, and I moved away to live in another part of the country with my mother and six-year-old sister, *forever.* Or so I thought. In an act of valor or sheer, self-immolating recklessness (I still have trouble telling which is which), I sat down and penned a letter. I don't remember exactly what I wrote, but I'm guessing the gist of it was "You are quiet, smart, and nice. I love you." Forever turned out to be about nine months. My parents reconciled, and I returned to my hometown to begin fifth grade at my old elementary school in September, with all my former classmates.

A gentleman in possession of such a letter might write back, thanking the tender lady for the compliment. He might rail against cursed destiny that he could not return her affections. He might gallantly deflect her indiscretion with an excuse: "I'm gay/engaged/sworn to the priesthood" are all serviceable white lies in such an instance.

David O'Neill did not do with my letter as a gentleman might. He did not do as my own nine-year-old son would most likely do, which is shrug, toss it in the trash, and go back to playing Star Wars. David O'Neill did the very thing a girl dreads most. He took the letter to school and showed everyone. My reputation never recovered.

I can't imagine any of my sons engaged in those dramas. Even my fifth-grader still seems oblivious to romantic love. And though in his case I expect that to change any day, as far as I can tell, they are completely incurious about sex. This is a merciful reprieve, since I am completely inept at explaining it to them. I resort to metaphors and similes that undoubtedly leave them more confused. One time we were baking a cake, and I used the cracking of eggs as a segue to a discussion of human reproduction. Consequently, my youngest still refers to his birthday as the day he "hatched." In trying to simplify sex, I make it needlessly complicated. Explaining homosexuality, I employed a metaphor of right- and left-handedness. Just as people are born preferring the use of one hand over the other, I told them, people are attracted to one gender over another.

"Understand?"

"If you're left-handed, you're gay?"

"Let me sort it out," a bisexual friend offered afterward. "I'm ambidextrous."

Maybe I'd do better with girls, but I doubt it. One of the reasons I'm so bad at giving "The Talk" is that I never received it myself. I learned about sex from reading my dad's *Penthouse* magazines, my mom's Nancy Friday books, and several hippie-era sexual health classics, including the hirsute original *Joy of Sex*. I learned about puberty from Judy Blume, and birth control from an ex-nun at my Catholic junior high school, who gave us dire warnings about the potential toxicity of latex. I have Bradley Wilburn to thank for introducing me to my clitoris, in sixth grade, when he accidentally found it during a tickle fight. We dated a few times in high school, but he had—disappointingly—forgotten where it was by then.

It wasn't that my parents were prudes. Far from it. Nudity figured prominently in our house, both in art and in life, to my complete mortification when friends came over to play early on a Saturday morning, and were treated to the sight of my father wandering bleary-eyed and stark naked from his bedroom to the toilet. Erotic literature could be found on the living room bookshelves beside the Tom Robbins and Erica Jong paperbacks, and I knew where to open to the X-rated parts of those books, too.

My mother worked at the local feminist resource center, and I had free range of the library there, which rounded out my formal education. I wasn't sheltered from sex, but I don't remember my parents addressing it openly with me, beyond slipping me a pamphlet or two and asking if I had any questions. I used to think it was strange that they, of all people, would be uncomfortable discussing sex, until I had my own kids. There's got to be a biological explanation for why this is so hard; an evolutionary advantage gained from it being uncomfortable to think about sex while looking at our offspring. It requires us to engage opposite parts of the brain simultaneously, like trying to write with both hands at the same time. I guess it does help to be ambidextrous.

Because my sons are all still in elementary school and aren't overtly curious about sex, it's easy to lull myself into believing that there's still plenty of time to make sure all the bases are covered before they start thinking about making it to any of them. But that's bound to be naive of me. When I consider how thoroughly acquainted I was with the contents of *my* parents' dresser drawers, I wonder what they've seen already, and if they understand it, or if they think it's strange that Mom keeps a light saber rolled up in her lingerie. Even if they really aren't that curious yet themselves, they go to school with girls, and some of them are bound to be girls like I was: *very* curious.

My firstborn is not that many years removed from the age I was when I first had sex, or the boy I first had sex with. I was very young, and my parents must have also assumed there would be plenty of time. Of course, I had to write the experience down, and of course, they found it and read it, and were beside themselves. But I was more precocious than promiscuous. Until my senior year, when I began what would be my first long-term relationship,

I had sex only a few times, none of it very memorable outside of whatever romantic drama I scripted in my imagination. I was somewhat careful, and mostly lucky, not to get pregnant before I meant to, at twenty-eight.

I've been ready, for years, with my argument for why any daughter of mine should wait several years longer than I did to have sex, which is simply that sex wasn't very good until I got older. It's like opening a wine too soon, I would tell her. Uninteresting, at best. *Give yourself a few more years. It will be much better then.* I could deliver that speech with the full authority of one who knew. But I don't know if it applies to young men. A man is better at sex when he's twenty-five than when he's seventeen, but I can't say that he's enjoying it more. The argument might not carry the same weight with a boy.

It's all I've got, though, so I'm going to give it to them anyway, and hope that my sons turn out to have a bit more sense and patience than their mother. And just in case reason doesn't persuade them to act responsibly, I've got a backup speech prepared. It's the one where I explain that I spared them from infant circumcision so that they would come into maturity with all their manly nerves intact. And that I've got until their eighteenth birthdays to change my mind.

I've gotten so comfortable not having other females in the family, it's easy to forget that I'll almost certainly have to make room for some before very much longer. Though I know it's desirable, healthy, and expected, I can't quite wrap my head around the idea of someone displacing me as the woman in my sons' lives. One of my friends claims that her mother-in-law's decision to surrender her son swiftly and graciously was key to a long and happy marriage between the couple and an enduring bond between the two women. I don't know if I have it in me to be that generous. What if I don't like the girl? What if she's all wrong for him? Wrong for me? She could be a he, but no matter who is cast as the romantic lead, I'll be moving off center stage. Which is as it should be. Though it melts my heart when my five-year-old says he wants to live with me forever, that's not how I want either of us to end up. It's just hard for him or me to picture it otherwise.

Of all my three sons, he is my most ardent loverboy. Obsessive, really. When he wants my attention, which is always, he puts his little hands on my cheeks and pulls my face in front of his to make sure I'm listening. If I happen to be sleeping, he will slap me a little first. It's less cute than it sounds at five in the morning. He was weaned at about fourteen months, but he is a dedicated boob man, and still cops a feel whenever he can. Fortunately, he can lay on the charm. "You look gorgeous!" he exclaims when he sees me with my head in curlers, getting ready to go out somewhere. "See how wet my eyes are," he say, accusingly, when I come back. "I missed you." He's intense. If he were my boyfriend, we'd have broken up long ago. And the restraining order would specifically state that he is not to come within five feet of my side of the bed between the hours of midnight and sunrise. As it is, he pretty much owns me.

But even he understands there are natural boundaries, proverbial spaces in our togetherness.

"Close your eyes," he has recently taken to ordering me when he's changing underwear. "I don't want you to see my wee-ness."

At five going on six, his wee-ness is under autonomous rule, no longer part of his mother's domain. And all the rest of him is lined up behind it, on the road to independence, or to another kind of allegiance.

Suppose the girl is great. Suppose we all love her, take her in as one of our own. Then suppose she breaks our hearts, or he breaks hers, what then?

My own parents suffered with me when my heart was broken, and suffered because of me, when I broke the heart of someone they'd come to love and regard as a member of the family. Once, after a fight with my boyfriend had ended badly, my misery so distressed my father that he personally intervened and negotiated a reconciliation on my behalf, without my knowledge. I never knew exactly how he brought it about, but my boyfriend came back early the next morning with a changed heart. The incredible part is, Daddy didn't even like that boyfriend much. But he could not stand to see his daughter in that particular kind of pain.

My mother and my first husband were close during the short time he and I were together, and when I confessed through tears that I had fallen in love with someone else, she hugged me hard, told me she loved me no matter what, and made it clear that her sympathy was with my home-wrecked husband. She knew that their relationship would atrophy on its own after a while, but she wasn't about to pull the plug before the love stopped flowing. It wasn't just about him and me, which is something I didn't appreciate until I had children of my own. Ever since they've been able to smile and make friends, I love whom they love. Even if I don't necessarily like them, or have anything in common with their mothers. The soccer field and playground make unlikely allies of us all. The mom of one of the kids' preschool friends once heard me mention something about going to church, and for two years, I let her go on thinking that I was a good fundamentalist Christian like she was, and not, as Patrick fondly describes us Episcopalians, a member of the church of freaks and queers. I was willing to let her believe I was saved as long as our sons were buddies. I would probably try to win back a girlfriend for him, too, even if *she* were a fundamentalist Christian. I'm invested in their relationships. And it's not that easy to withdraw the investment just because the principal players have moved on.

It's unrealistic to hope that my children won't ever get divorced, given the statistics, and their own parents' history, but I hope it anyway. It's easy to get a divorce, but it's hard to get unmarried, even when the cut is clean and bloodless, like mine was. Our legal and financial ties were easily dissolved, and there were no children to keep us connected to each other. I moved away, and apart from a split-second, chance sighting across a parking lot during a summer vacation over ten years ago, we never saw each other again. Even so, the severed life is a phantom limb that sometimes twitches and aches for no apparent cause. It's been nearly fifteen years since I kissed that husband good-bye—three times as many years apart as we were a couple—but sometimes I still dream about him; that we are together in the home we once shared, and that it's this life that's been the dream all along.

Most of the time, my memory of him is distant and unfocused, a face in the background. But then something will bring it into sudden focus. Once it was a silver locket, tarnished and forgotten at the bottom of my jewelry box. Inside, our two portraits were still hinged together, each of them so small it was like spying through the wrong end of a telescope. A stolen backward glance. Sometimes it's my oldest son who reminds me of him, lean and tall, with his sandy brown hair and blue eyes, his innate esprit de corps and love of order. It's ironic to glimpse traces of the life I left behind in the life I ran toward, and it could be pure projection, yet it moves me when I see the similarities. Nothing is ever really lost.

There's no reason for those memories and dreams to occasionally haunt me. As far as I'm aware, I have no unfinished business with that long-ago part of my history. Except that I think, on some level, maybe there is no divorce. Maybe if you make those vows, you don't get your whole deposit back. Parts of your souls stay tangled up together, for better or for worse. I mean to tell my boys that, too, before I blink and they're men already, picking out rings, making promises that are impossible to keep and hard to take back. But the metaphysics of love will have to wait until I've covered the mechanics. You know, the basic facts. Like where eggs come from when both chickens are left-handed.

# 14.

# Mom, the Musical

Whenever career counselors try to parlay child-rearing experience into marketable job skills, what they typically come up with are administrative functions, like appointment making and record keeping. As if you'd want to do those things for anyone to whom you weren't legally or morally bound. They completely overlook the far more specialized skill set moms acquire over the course of those years, which easily qualifies many of us for top creative positions at Disney World, or in Broadway musical theater. By the time our kids head off to college, we are show business veterans, having produced, directed, and starred in such classics as "Christmas," "Halloween," "Birthday Party" and other holiday extravaganzas for eighteen consecutive years, at breathless tempo. Motherhood isn't a desk job. It's vaudeville.

Let's take a run through the standard repertoire. Practically speaking, the first major production of the year is Valentine's Day. Chronologically, it should be New Year's, but that's an adult-oriented occasion, which properly belongs to the child-free, since they can sleep in the next morning. They're welcome to it. The rest of us can't stay awake till midnight anymore, anyway.

Valentine's Day used to involve champagne and debauchery, too, but classroom party preparations leave a mother too exhausted for romance. V-Day is the biggest classroom party of the school year, and conscription into its service is impossible to avoid. I have three elementary school kids who have up to thirty classmates each. That's a lot of love to deliver. I'm usually up late the night before, hot-gluing foil-wrapped chocolate hearts to cards, signing X's and O's, cutting sandwiches into heart shapes, and hating everyone. I think mothers wearing a school visitor name tag on February 14 should be treated like military veterans, with drinks on the house and complimentary manicures wherever we go.

When I was a kid, about a thousand years ago, Valentine's Day was all about the valentines, which were painstakingly hand-cut from a book that contained not one licensed, trademarked character. You chose the plainest, slightly backhanded ones for the kids you didn't like, and the most ornate, gushing ones for the kids you did, and we gave it to each other straight up, without the orgiastic euphoria of corn syrup solids to cloud things. For party refreshments, we had our own tender, young hearts to eat out. I don't know when that changed, or whether it's an American thing, but every valentine my kids give and receive comes attached to at least one piece of candy. As if that didn't add up to enough insulin resistance, the room moms mix up a vat of sugar and red food dye and pour it in a feed trough. Or they might as well, considering what is actually served. If you've seen video montages of psychedelic "happenings" in the sixties, you've seen something like a modern Valentine's Day classroom party. On the glycemic disaster index, Valentine's is second only to Halloween.

I try to limit my on-site presence to dropping a snack off at the door and running, but this year I thought I'd linger and check in on my third-grader's class. The party couldn't have been going more than twenty minutes, but the floor and desktops were already littered with red and pink cellophane wrappers. My child was slumped backward in his seat in what appeared to be a diabetic coma. Several empty Pixy Stix tubes lay scattered in front of him. His lips twitched slightly when I spoke his name. About half his classmates were also catatonic at their desks. The other half were doing gymnastics across the room. Their drug dealers, the room moms, stood paralyzed against the wall, as if watching a fire they had accidentally started.

"Here," I said to my son, picking up a bottle of spring water from a treat bag and silently blessing whichever mother had thoughtfully included it in the loot. "I think you should drink some of this."

He rallied enough to unscrew the bottle top and pour in a packet of red drink mix that had come with it. Of course. I eased out the door, hoping he would hit his bottom and find a recovery program before the bell rang.

Sugar is to children's parties as cocaine is to the entertainment industry. If your kid is part of the scene, you have to accept that they're going to come into contact with it. You hope for the best, and brace for the worst. For a very short while, I thought I could keep my babies' pancreases pristine. I kept them away from refined carbohydrates. I limited fruit juice. I made them barley-sweetened whole grain teething biscuits that even the dog wouldn't eat. But I couldn't keep it up. The slope of my nutritive backslide can be plotted by each of my kid's first birthday cakes. When the oldest turned one, I made him a whole wheat carrot cake with pineapple-sweetened cream cheese on top. Two years later, it was a homemade chocolate layer cake, frosted with buttercream, for my middle child. Three years after that, I ran by the warehouse club and picked up a slab of corn syrup and hydrogenated vegetable oil, spray-painted blue, for the baby.

It was an increasingly futile effort anyway, since we don't live in a bubble. Even the bank tellers at the drive-up window are pushing candy. School is just a high-fructose corn syrup distribution hub. I've had to shift from a preventative focus to damage control. I can't keep my kids from getting their hands on a can of soda when they leave our house, but I can at least make sure they've had something nutritious before they get out the door. I figure it's better to shoot for moderation anyway. I grew up under a very strict anti-junk-food regime, and wiped out all seventeen years of it in one semester of college. My husband, on the other hand, grew up with no dietary rules or restrictions, and never developed an internal regulator to suggest that there should ever be any. Outside of the suppers I cook, he eats like a twelve-year-old with no mother. So I've relaxed my standards in hopes of finding the middle way.

Besides, what's childhood without an occasional sugar buzz? At least once in your life, I figure, you've got to eat a chocolate bunny the size of your head, and you might as well do it when you can most efficiently metabolize it. I must have a little bit of the pusher in me. I loved watching each of my kids realize for the first time what's inside a plastic Easter egg, what comes after they say "trick or treat."

"HAPPY BIRTHDAY TO ME," my youngest bellowed joyfully up and down the street, the first year he could trick-or-treat on his own two feet and hold his loot bag by himself.

Where creative output is concerned, Halloween is an even bigger production than Valentine's Day. It's also more competitive. Everyone's in it to win for best costume design and best front porch special effects. To add to the intensity, there's almost always a conflict between directors and actors as to whose artistic vision should get prime consideration. The actors in our house always win. My cute and original costume suggestions are consistently rejected in favor of the trademarked and cliché.

"Ninjas, again?" I ask, when presented with their demands. "That's so 2005. What about the headless man I showed you?"

"It's weird."

"It's *avant-garde*."

Actors.

Halloween is just as much, or more, work for me, as any of the other major kids' holidays, but I get to share in the fun to a greater extent than at Valentine's Day or Easter. For starters, there is the kickback from the treat bags. I prefer to take my cut in chocolate, but will also accept candy corn and caramels. And then there are the grown-up parties, with the excuse to dress up, something I love to do. My husband loves it considerably less.

In fact, no two words strung together will strike dread into his heart, and joy into mine, like "theme" and "party." The last time I persuaded him to put a costume on, we were going to an all-ages gathering, and I came across a cheeky, last-minute concept he agreed was too apt to resist. I folded and pinned a tablecloth around him like a giant diaper and dropped a couple of onions down the back so it would sag appropriately. When we arrived at the party, the adults immediately caught on that he was a—wait for it—party pooper. We were basking in the glow of a well-delivered punch line, when someone's little boy wandered into the room, carrying a plate of cookies.

"Hey," Patrick said to him, in that overbright tone that adults use with children sometimes. "Do you know what I am?" To make it easier on the kid, I made a sweeping, game show hostess gesture toward my husband's rear end.

The little boy looked at me and then back at Patrick with enormous, solemn brown eyes, and made his best guess.

"An ass?"

Theme parties are a curious custom of the married-with-children set. It's as if we're all lost at sea on a twenty-year cruise, and have to keep our spirits up. Or it could be that they serve an important psychological function, helping us to shed old identities that no longer fit. How else could you appropriately say good-bye to your leather jeans and rollerblades? There are costume parties, dance parties, karaoke parties, bad Santa parties, taco parties, pool parties. Over one Christmas holiday, I attended three separate "tacky sweater" parties. I think I developed an allergy to acrylic yarn that year.

Occasionally, single people are drawn into one of these events: someone's bachelor neighbor, or visiting younger sister, persuaded to come in from the cold world outside and warm themselves in the glow of string lights and thinly suppressed marital tensions. Oddly, they never seem to come back.

For kids, the ultimate theme party is, of course, the birthday party. In the annual scheme of things, it's the big showstopper. The other holidays follow a pretty standard arrangement from year to year. You go to the attic, pull out the appropriately labeled boxes, and take it from there. But every single birthday party starts from scratch. You have to determine the theme, select a venue, compile the guest list, plan the activities, coordinate the decor, and prepare a menu, all out of whole cloth. Smart planning starts before you even get pregnant, by arranging it so that your children are born in May or September, well spaced from other special occasions, and never in the same month as a sibling. Then you won't have to greet every New Year's Day with a scream because you just remembered you have two birthday parties to pull off in the next six days, and no money, time, or energy left with which to do it.

In the carefree, frisky days of spring, mating seems like a swell idea. Birds do it, bees do it, you think blithely as you yield to the primal rutting urge, humming a Cole Porter tune. Forty weeks later, sometime between hosting Thanksgiving dinner and dismantling the holiday decor, you will remember that birds and bees fly away and leave their young, Cole Porter was gay and childless, and that you are the one stuck hosting birthday parties at the worst possible time of the year. When my two older boys, born in the first week of January, two years apart, were very small, the timing of their birthdays wasn't quite so inconvenient. Before they got wise to the calendar, not only was it possible to postpone the party for weeks, I could get away with a joint celebration. But all that changed once the first went off to school and saw that other kids were having birthday parties near, or even on, their actual birthdays, and didn't have to share the billing. The bar was raised, early and high.

With three kids in grade school, the number of birthday party invitations we receive is staggering. There have been weekends when all I seem to do is ferry kids from one party to another, sometimes as many as three in one day, which thrice exceeds the quota established by the Council for Not Losing Your Freaking Mind. The mileage alone is exorbitant. The home birthday party seems to be all but extinct, with celebrations held at the newest inflatables/bowling/gymnastics facility, usually in an industrial park on the outskirts of town. I am sure if I added up the fuel cost times three kids at fourteen years each, I would do just as well to buy a trailer and make our weekend home the parking lot of whatever party spot is this season's must-rent.

Most of those places are pretty horrible, but none so nerve-shattering as Chuck E. Cheese, the indoor kiddie arcade/restaurant with the creepy animatronics. Kids love it, parents hate it. I dread seeing Chuck E.'s sneering face turn up in our mailbox.

Nothing says clean, safe, and child-friendly like a snaggletooth rat wearing a baseball cap, gang style. The strolling, in-house version of the mascot is terrifying. It looks like it carries plague. "If that rodent comes over here," I heard one toddler's father whisper to another across a party table, "I'm taking him out."

To be fair, my kids love to attend those outsourced parties, and from time to time, we've hosted one. But to me they feel antisocial. The activity level doesn't allow the kids to really connect, and the turnstile format doesn't let them practice much in the way of social graces. Instead of getting to play guests and hosts, and focusing on each other, such parties tend to be all about the action. I jumped off that bandwagon early, declaring myself a one-mom society for the preservation and advancement of the simple, homemade party. These have struck some of our guests as so exotic, it feels like it *is* the theme. "What a *neat* idea!" one mother exclaimed, when she dropped off her son and was told we'd be staying put and playing some bingo and musical chairs.

Another time, we had a camping-out party in the backyard. "Is that a *stick*?" shouted one of the little boys, as I explained in my chirpiest camp director voice that we'd be roasting hot dogs and marshmallows. He made gagging noises. "I don't think I can eat food on a *stick*!"

He could, and did, and loved it. My kids were in private school at the time, with the help of scholarship funds made possible by wealthy families like the one that boy belonged to. It was a very good, very expensive school, and we felt lucky to be there. But after that night, I began to think the benefits flowed both ways, that some of those kids were lucky to have us, too.

The key to a homemade party is to keep it simple, or you may as well hire it out. As a Google of do-it-yourself birthday party ideas will swiftly demonstrate, it can be all too easy to get carried away. I recommend not even looking at the websites. You'll be stenciling monograms onto hand-sewn favor bags and airbrushing fondant. The handmade movement is supposed to be an alternative to conspicuous consumption, but sometimes I think it's just a sneakier way of showing off.

Who are we knocking ourselves out trying to impress, anyway? The birthday kid? Mine would love a three-ring circus in the backyard, but they don't really care what the theme or venue is, as long as they can get together with their friends, eat cake, and open presents. The party guests? I've yet to meet a child who wasn't perfectly delighted with a few rounds of stick-the-tail on something and a helium balloon to take home. For sure, we're not doing it to impress the dads ("What—is it someone's birthday?"). The applause of other moms is what we're after. A birthday party is an exhibition for us as much as it is an amusement for the kids. We use it to communicate how affluent or frugal we are, how offbeat or mainstream, how socially or environmentally conscious, how creative and capable. It has become a statement; our float in the parade.

We *should* applaud each other. Not for best in show, or showing off, but just for showing up. With heart-shaped sandwiches and store-bought cookies. With shamrocks made of twist ties to ward off pinches when all the green clothes are dirty. With dozens upon dozens of plastic eggs filled in the wee hours, whether with jelly beans or nuts and raisins. With our hands full of pumpkin guts. With our minds full of dollars and cents as we help write letters to Santa. With nothing to say for ourselves when we remember what we were supposed to bring to class that day, and forgot. With a candle for every blessed year, and the wish that we could grant every single wish.

We should all hold hands, and take a bow. There's no business like it.

# 15

# Mommy Wears Prada

I'm in the bathroom at the Prada store in New York City having a bit of a moment. I thought it would be a good place to sit in private and get some perspective. And it might be, except all four walls are mirrored from floor to ceiling. Now, in addition to hyperventilating over the fact that I am wearing more than a thousand dollars' worth of designer clothes, I'm a little freaked out by having to watch myself reflected into infinity. I've fallen into an alternative universe.

I'm a soccer mom. A den mom. I clip coupons. How did I get here?

I was reading a magazine article, and the next thing I knew, I was in it.

A few weeks prior to my Prada moment, a magazine in the

checkout lane tempted me with the suggestion that life could be simpler and easier—so I tossed it in the cart with my preschooler and the load of groceries that *might* get our family of five through the next two days. It was a week or two later before I managed to barricade myself in the bathroom, sink into a bubble bath, and flip through the issue.

"Wardrobe Staples" caught my eye. I am a mother of three. Getting out the door without peanut-butter smears on my yoga pants is an achievement. Looking pulled together on a daily basis is the mythical holy grail. I eagerly turned to the article.

Classic pumps: $495 . . . Classic diamond studs: $5,000 . . . Classic trench coat: $1,395. I could afford the $24 classic tank top, but it would have to wait until my husband got paid again.

I added up the list. Ten grand. More than twice our monthly income.

Remember the scene in *The Devil Wears Prada* where Anne Hathaway, playing the ingenue intern at a high-fashion magazine, smirks over an intense editorial discussion about couture? That's not me. I am not above fashion. I recognize that real artistry goes into the design and manufacture of fine clothing, and that there is a market for it. But it mystifies me when it is marketed to moms like me. If the editors of these lists were to leave Manhattan and come to Little Rock, Arkansas, to stand behind me in the supermarket line, coupon book in hand, would they tap me on the shoulder and tell me that a $2,000 designer handbag was an "essential"?

I've read the arguments. That bag, those shoes, that dress, will last a lifetime if properly cared for. They will never go out of style. They are an investment.

Really? *Really?*

I honestly wondered. I thought about my gray cashmere sweater, a gift from my mother. At $100, it's one of the most expensive garments I've ever owned. Putting it on always makes me feel like a million bucks. I had to admit, that was a pretty good return. Would slipping into a pair of $500 Manolo Blahniks make me feel so confident, so sexy, so put-together that it would be worth going without cable TV for a year? I didn't know. But I sure wished I could find out.

The kids were clamoring at the bathroom door. I let the magazine fall to the floor. My wish should have popped with the last soap bubble, but the next day I e-mailed an editor at *Good Housekeeping* with a challenge: Let an average mom test-drive some of these "must-have" clothes in real life and decide just how essential they are. As my nine-year-old son would say, I double-dog-dared them.

A month later, I got a message on my voice mail: When could I come to New York to go shopping?

⚘

When you enter Hearst Tower on the corner of West 57th Street, you are met with a waterfall that spans three-quarters the width of the marble lobby. A diagonal bank of escalators conveys an endless cascade of magazine workers, who ascend and descend with big-city assurance and poise.

And the woman with the giant purple suitcase, stuck in the revolving door? That would be me.

After a very nice security guard rescues me, a *Good House-*

*keeping* staffer takes me upstairs, and in a glass-paneled conference room, high above Manhattan, the editors and I review The
List: commonly agreed-upon "classic" wardrobe items that I am
to purchase and take home for a reality test. I look it over. They
are the must-haves I've been told all my adult life I must have. I
have a generous budget and a town car with a driver at my disposal for the next three days. My kids are home in Little Rock
with my husband and my mother for the week. Magically, we've
already bypassed several significant obstacles to a middle-income
mom looking to dress herself from the must-have list: geography,
child care, money, and parking.

I am not complaining.

My first stop is Prada on Madison Avenue. Reuben, my driver,
pulls up to the sidewalk in front of the store, walks around, and
opens my door. I step out and face the wide glass entrance with
its brass fixtures and elegant lettering. At least it's not a revolving
door.

I enter the store like a scared little girl on the first day of kindergarten. A beautiful young woman named Christina comes
over, smiling. I tell her I am looking to purchase a few classic
wardrobe pieces. She asks me several questions about my taste
and lifestyle, and listens attentively. She points out fabrics and
construction details of garments as if I were buying a car or
a sofa. I nod yes to this, no to that. Eventually, she leads me
to a sitting area where there are dressing rooms. Someone brings
a bottle of Perrier and a crystal tumbler on a linen-lined tray,
and sets it down on the white leather ottoman. Would I like a
cappuccino?

Toto, we're not in Kmart anymore.

The first item I try on is a pair of black trousers in a light-weight fabric I am told is wool crepe. I can tell right away there is something different about them. They feel amazing. When I look in the mirror, I gasp. I turn around and around. My rear end has instantly lost five pounds and ten years. My belly looks flatter. I think I am having a religious experience. Christina finds me a pair of pumps to try with them. A soft-spoken woman with an Italian accent comes and pins the trousers to the right length for the heel height. They'll be hemmed and ready for me that day. It all seems to be included in the price.

I'm in Prada for nearly two hours. In addition to the trousers, I buy a black pencil skirt. Christina leaves me to finish my cappuccino and brings me a discreet sales slip on a lacquered tray, like a restaurant check. I wish the supermarket operated like this.

"I think you're a Prada girl," says Christina, as we hug good-bye. I think she's right.

Over the next forty-eight hours, I shop up and down Madison and Fifth Avenues. I decide that Reuben the Driver is my New York husband. He drives me to stores, opens my door, waits for me outside for hours without complaint, and never once nags me about how much I'm spending.

My fears of being treated shabbily by shop staff are mostly unfounded. One exception is an Italian woolens boutique, where the cold shoulder I receive colors my perception of the wares. The cashmere sweaters seem ridiculously overpriced and too fragile for the constant tug of little hands. There's no way around it, though. Cashmere is a perennial on every staples list. I reluctantly go with a cream scoop-neck pullover with ribbed sleeves that feel somewhat substantial. It's undeniably beautiful, but I have a hard time signing the receipt for $730. I can tell it is a better sweater than the one my mother gave me, but there's no way it's seven times better.

At Manolo Blahnik, I have to ring a bell to be let in. Inside, people are coming unglued. The scene reminds me of the giant candy store on the Upper East Side I visited a few days before. There's a woman talking to herself in a corner, surrounded by discarded shoes she's tried on. There's a thirteen-year-old sulking on a chair while multiple generations of her family negotiate with her over heel height. Most shocking, shoppers are shoving their bare feet into the shoes. Every Payless or JCPenney customer is expected to sheathe her foot in a disposable sockette before trying something on, but apparently not in Manolo Blahnik.

It's true what they say: The rich are not like you and me.

I tell a saleswoman I am looking for a pair of classic black pumps. I'm thinking a black pump is a black pump, but apparently not. She converts my American shoe size (in all the stores where I shop, sizing is European), and selects three or four pairs in varying heel heights, cuts, and textures. A shiny black patent leather pair twinkles at me. I try them on and stand up. I am a hundred feet tall, a supermodel–rock star. "I'll take them."

Outside, I check the list. I've shopped Prada, Chanel, Loro Piana, Yves Saint Laurent, Gucci, Christian Louboutin, Manolo Blahnik, and Burberry. I have a pencil skirt, trousers, a trench coat, pumps, sunglasses—all in black—the cashmere sweater, skinny jeans from Saks, and a red silk scarf from a lovely lady at Hermès who could teach my Cub Scout den a thing or two about tying knots.

I have to decide about a bag.

The budget I've been given for this shopping spree allows

$2,000 for an "It" bag. I'm conflicted on two counts here. Two thousand dollars is nearly twice my mortgage payment. It's five times my monthly utility bills. It's a whole lot of things my husband and I have had to put off or forgo when the money just wasn't there.

Then there's the "It" word. "It" means a status symbol. "It" means standing out. "It" means a bunch of things that aren't really me.

I liked the quiet black bag I saw at Prada and an equally discreet tan bag at Yves Saint Laurent. If I can get beyond the price, those are more my style. But this story isn't just about me. I feel like I'm here on behalf of every mom like me who ever wondered from her bathtub what all the hype over a brand of shoes or bag was all about. In this case, I have to go for the hype.

I tell Reuben, "Louis Vuitton, please."

At the store, the famous LV monogram seems to be on every item in stock. I ask the sales associate to show me the tote styles. If I have to spend $2,000 on a bag, it had better hold my laptop. There's one with a lot of brass hardware on it that seems a little flashy for my taste. But I like its generous size, and the shoulder strap is a good length for me.

The new bag costs more than $1,500 with tax added. I hand over my debit card, holding my breath. Even though I warned my bank in Little Rock to expect some unusual charges this week, I keep expecting the card to catch fire.

The purse I am wearing was a free replacement for a $30 purse that fell apart in two weeks, given begrudgingly after I persuaded the store manager that its life expectancy should have been at least a couple of months. I bet I've owned at least fifty bags of similar quality over the last twenty years. The idea of investing in a few expensive pieces that will last doesn't seem so unreasonable.

Mission accomplished.

The total damage: nearly six thousand dollars.

Waiting for my driver to take me back to my hotel, I see a poorly dressed man struggling across the intersection in a wobbly old wheelchair. In the shop behind me, there are $30,000 handbags, and a three-year waiting list to buy one. There's the perspective I was looking for.

It's time to go home and see how these clothes really fit.

similar quality over the last twenty years.

"That's the ugliest purse I've ever seen," my husband blurts out, when I show him the bag.

I'm slightly wounded. I'm still not entirely comfortable with its brass plaque etched with the brand name (in case the monogrammed initials are too subtle). But it's undeniably a classic, and the large tote size works. I transfer the contents of my old purse—my wallet, a jumbo tube of baby sunscreen, a Ziploc bag of Goldfish crackers, my coupon file—and toss in my beat-up laptop. It all fits.

My husband wants to know what it cost.

"Fifteen hundred dollars," I tell him.

"That's insane."

"You better learn to like it, you'll be seeing it for a long while."

He spots the shoe box. "Show me the shoes."

I kick off my mom clogs and slip barefoot into the black patent Manolos. The shoes have a three-and-a-half-inch heel.

"Six hundred dollars," I say.

My husband is staring at my feet, mouth agape.

"I'm totally okay with that," he says.

I'm timid, at first, about wearing my new things in public. I start with the Gucci sunglasses, on a play date at the park. They cost $300 and have plastic frames with plastic lenses, just like every other pair of sunglasses I've ever owned. At the park, they are a nonevent. If anyone notices them at all, they probably assume they are knockoffs. I don't know which is worse: to be considered extravagant or a sucker.

The next day, I wear the Prada skirt with a long-sleeve T-shirt from Target and a pair of low-heeled sandals. Around noon, I take my preschooler to the library and grocery store. I take the "It" bag with me.

My preschooler remarks, "You have a new purse."

"Yes," I say.

"It's so *shiny*," he says.

Exactly.

"Shiny, shiny, pretty, pretty," he sings the entire way into the store.

The cashier thinks so, too. "I love your bag," she calls out to me as I wheel my cart away.

"Thanks." I smile back at her with genuine pleasure.

The first friend to call me out on a label is Alisha. It's Moms' Night Out and five of us are carpooling to a nightclub to hear a Latin band. When Alisha climbs in the back row with me, she notices the bag.

"*Nice* Louis Vuitton!" she exclaims. Everyone turns around. "Is it real?"

Blushing, I tell her it is, and there ensues a hilarious debate in the parking lot as to whether it is more hassle to take "Louie" inside the club with us and worry about someone taking it, or to hide it in the van outside and worry about someone breaking in.

"I don't believe this!" Alisha says with mock irritation. "It's like you dragged along one of your kids!"

We decide to bring "Louie" inside and take turns keeping an eye on it.

"If you see anyone besides me leave with this bag," I tell the doorman, "tackle them."

I'm joking, but the bag causes real worry. I'm hopelessly absentminded. One day I bring in groceries and forget the purse. My husband takes our van to a meeting, where he gets a frantic text message from me: "THERE IS A $1,500 BAG IN THE VAN. GO GET IT NOW."

The burden of privilege.

Over time, the bag begins to feel more natural to me. I love its size and its durability. I don't feel afraid to handle it, the way I do the cashmere sweater or the Hermès scarf.

Gradually, the clothes are integrated into my life. I get a lot of mileage from the Prada pencil skirt, dressed up and down. I discover that the scarf looks great as a belt for my jeans, though I have to take it off when it starts to rain. I wear the trousers only twice before they need to go to the dry cleaner, an errand that seems to stay at the bottom of the to-do list. Maintenance is definitely going to be an issue.

The Manolos go as easily to third-grade chapel as to a dinner party, where I indulge in my most flagrant act of label flashing.

I'm standing in a circle of women, when one of them looks down and gushes, "Great shoes!" I'm about to say, "Thank you," when I realize she is talking about the shoes next to mine. "Thanks," says the person for whom the compliment was intended. "I got them at that vintage store. I love yours!"

"You do? I got these online somewhere."

*Oh, for heaven's sake.* The two women are comparing shoe sizes, so I reach down and remove one shoe on the pretense of having forgotten what mine is. The label is clearly printed on the inside. "Manolos!" one of the women gasps.

Finally.

But the real moment of reckoning comes one evening when I have to run out last-minute to the grocery store. It's been a typical, nonstop day, and I'm wiped out. My hair is dirty. I'm in old jeans and a T-shirt. I can't believe I have to go out in public. Then I remember the black Burberry trench coat.

I throw it on. The Louis Vuitton bag slips easily over my shoulder. I slide the Gucci sunglasses over my head. It's magic. Instantly I look, and feel, like someone who has it together. Isn't that worth a few thousand bucks?

Heck, yeah—if you've got a few thousand to burn. Of course, if it all turned to discount at the stroke of midnight, I would feel a mighty pang, but nothing more serious than that. As they say, it's just fashion, darling.

The keeper, the real must-have, is that woman I kept running into all over New York City: the one standing a hundred feet tall and fabulous in the mirror every time I turned around. The woman who's allowed as much time as she needs to discover what she wants. The one who walks confidently through doors that are opened for her and is free to enjoy beautiful unnecessary things without the fear that she's losing her soul. The one who can dream up things that are wildly impossible from the bathtub and watch them come true.

If it takes wearing something special on the outside to remind me I am always her on the inside, I think that's okay. You can call it an investment. But it isn't in the clothes.

16.

# Me, the People

"Give me your tired, your poor,
Your huddled masses yearning to breathe free,
The wretched refuse of your teeming shore.
Send these, the homeless, tempest-tost to me,
I lift my lamp beside the golden door!"

—Excerpt from "The New Colossus" by EMMA LAZARUS,
inscribed on a plaque inside the Statue of Liberty

I was tired, wretched, and yearning to breathe free the first time I knocked timidly on America's golden door, but America did not lift her lamp to me. Instead, I was escorted to a waiting room beyond the U.S. Customs inspection area of Toronto's international airport, and told to take a seat. An enormous wall plaque dominated the room, depicting a stern bald eagle that looked like it might swoop down and eat me. I sank into my chair and watched the clock as minutes passed and the hour changed. My flight departure time came and went without me, and with it went the last frayed wisps of my courage. By the time I was ushered into an interview room by a customs officer, I was ready to click my heels together however many times it took to get back home.

My Canadian passport and visitor information form lay on the desk between us. He picked them up and reviewed the facts that had flagged me in the preclearance line as undesirable and unwelcome. One, I was traveling on a one-way ticket, purchased that morning by an American friend. Two, I had no idea how long I intended to stay with said friend. Three, I had no cash with me, and I had been unemployed for several months, as had my friend. Four, I was clearly a nervous wreck. The only thing separating me from the usual suspects was that I hadn't made any attempt at all to conceal or minimize the damning evidence against me. But it hadn't occurred to me that I should. I was twenty-five years old, and the only time I had traveled outside Canada as an adult was for my Jamaican honeymoon, two years before. I had no idea that my circumstances would flag me as a would-be illegal immigrant. When my hands and voice shook as I handed over my passport for inspection, it wasn't because I was scared of getting caught, but because I was in the middle of coming completely unglued. I was going to America just long enough to figure out my next move. I didn't want to *live* there. Why would anyone? The news made it sound like a stupid, scary place to be.

*That's a Canadian passport, pal,* I felt like saying to the officious clerk, who was looking smug, as if he'd foiled my schemes. *I'm not some refugee.*

Except I *was* a refugee, fleeing a comfortable life that had recently become intolerable, thanks to the catastrophe of falling in love with an American. Patrick would be waiting for my plane to arrive in Little Rock, watching the last passenger come through the gate, telling himself I was coming on the next flight. Champagne and a vase of flowers in a hotel room. The long night.

The interviewing officer turned to his computer keyboard, poised to enter my name in a database of the huddled masses. There wasn't going to be another flight for me. Not headed in that direction. Maybe it was the clear sign I'd been seeking all these anguished months. Maybe I wouldn't feel so defeated if I just surrendered.

"I left my husband this morning," I said, quietly. "But I think I made a mistake."

He stared at me a long moment across his desk. Then, without saying a word, he slowly handed me back my passport, took me by the arm, and walked me back to the Canadian side of the airport. I made two phone calls from a bank of pay phones, then flew back to a life I desperately wanted to belong to, but didn't anymore. Homeless, and tempest-tost.

That miserable November day turned out to be the backward step it sometimes takes to make a giant leap. Three months later, legally separated, I joined Patrick in Mexico, and the following spring, accompanied him back to the United States, though I still had no intention of staying longer than was absolutely necessary. It was still a stupid, scary country as far as I was concerned. But bumming around with the other ex-pats in San Miguel de Allende wasn't paying the rent. If we saved carefully, we figured, Patrick could quickly earn enough USD to buy us a year or more of *la vida mexicana*. We promised all our friends we'd see them soon, gassed up the car, and drove north.

"Welcome to Texas," a road sign announced. It might as well have read "Here Be Dragons." Driving through the streets of Laredo, I felt like I'd left civilization behind. Hand-painted gas station signs advertised "GUNS BEER AMMO" as if it were the lunch special, beverage included. We pulled into a fast-food joint for supper, and I marveled at the grotesque portions, my first exposure to supersizing. I could barely grasp the soda cup with one hand, tucking it inside the crook of my elbow instead, like I was playing a bagpipe, not drinking a cola. We found a cheap motel and checked in. When Patrick said he was going out to buy cigarettes, I freaked out.

"It looks like a dangerous neighborhood," I said, fretfully.

"I'm just going around the corner," he reassured me.

But I meant the neighborhood that extended from the Mexican border all the way to Canada. As far as I knew from watching television, the entire citizenry of the United States was armed to the teeth, running around shooting each other over imported vehicles or a bad day at the post office. International media coverage of America tends to draw from extremes. I'd grown up with nightly news portrayals of a dystopian anarchy so violent it made Mad Max look like an Outward Bound adventure. I was frantic the entire fifteen minutes Patrick was gone, convinced he would be shot.

He came back unharmed, and the next day we set out across Texas, arriving in Little Rock two days later, without being shot at once. After several consecutive weeks passed without either of us getting mowed down in a hail of bullets, I began to relax and take in my new surroundings. In Mexico, I'd acquired an idle expatriate's taste for people-watching, and the dives we frequented in Little Rock offered a steady parade. It was a pageant of misfits and miscreants: drunks and drug addicts, rednecks and hippies, young strippers and old groupies, musicians who were on their way up and those who were all the way down, trust-fund kids who were slumming, and ghetto kids on the hustle. Everyone was a character. Fear gave away to detached bemusement, then exhilaration. I loved the freedom of being a stranger, an observer of the show. And what a show.

"This country is a train wreck," I wrote gleefully in a letter to my father during my first year in the United States. Maybe so, but I met it in a head-on collision. I became a connoisseur of trash culture, venturing out from the neighborhood bars in search of something even grittier. I found it in highway joints where you had to be ready to duck under the table when a brawl erupted, where everybody and their gun was always half cocked and fully loaded, and the possibility of getting shot was no paranoid delusion. I was playing a part. I drank bourbon, smoked Marlboros, got fake nails, and knotted my shirts below my breasts. I thought I was on TV. I thought I was Daisy Duke. I thought I was badass. Dumbass, more like. One night, after all the bars and even the strip clubs were closed, we wound up in somebody's house down a country road, where I picked up an antique pistol off a table and swung around brandishing it in a two-handed grip, posing like a Charlie's Angel. Everyone in the room ducked and shouted at me, and I was shocked by the response. It hadn't crossed my mind that the gun might be loaded, or that anyone on the business end of the barrel would think it was loaded. I had never held a pistol that wasn't a toy. As far as I was concerned, it was just a prop. Like so much about America, it seemed too far out to be real.

In those early days, it was a thrill just to sit in a diner booth at four in the morning, ordering a breakfast of biscuits and gravy from a gum-cracking waitress who called me "hon." The Waffle House was no less exotic to me than a sidewalk café on the Left

Bank or a tearoom in Japan. The giant American flags that flew over car dealerships and truck stops were as colloquial and curious to me as dharma banners fluttering on a mountainside in Nepal—expressions of a local faith, not mine.

Gradually, the novelty wore off. Our lifestyle changed. We never did make it back to San Miguel. Patrick got a desk job, we got an apartment, got married, bought a house, and had a bunch of children. No regrets. It was good to settle down. But every year I spend in this land of the free has cost me more of my freedom. I'm not an onlooker anymore. I don't relish it when things go off the rails. I have children on the train now, and many other people I care about. My heart heaves and shakes with every rumble of the track. I'm tied to it.

I might as well just get on board, but I've held off making that last leap. My passport is still Canadian. Most people assume I'm a U.S. citizen. But to a careful observer, there are a few signs that should give me away. The Pledge of Allegiance is one. At the request to "please stand," I rise to my feet along with everyone else, out of respect. I put my hand over my heart like everyone else does, out of affection. And then I just stand there, mutely smiling and trying not to appear seditious while the rest of the assembly pledges fealty to the flag and the republic for which it stands. No one has ever once turned to me afterward and called me a traitor, or asked me what I'm protesting, but the self-consciousness and anxiety I endure for those two minutes is acute. *I'm Canadian,* I telegraph silently through my smile. *Don't shoot.*

"I'm Canadian," I explain, in an apologetic aside to whoever happens to be standing next to me, as soon as they get through "justice for all." They are always amazed, as if just learning that there is such a place. "Oh! Canada!" they exclaim, whenever

I out myself. Nine out of ten people will then say something nice about Vancouver, a city four thousand miles away from my East Coast hometown. I've never been anywhere near there, but when I go, I will have a lot of kind words to pass on, and numerous distant relatives of Americans to look up.

"I had no idea you were Canadian," they say next, if we've been coming to Scouts together for a while, or passing each other coming and going in the school hallways. *Living and breeding in your very midst,* I think, as they scan me for any visible marker of foreignness that hitherto escaped them.

In Mexico, the other ex-pats used to joke that the only way to tell a Canadian apart from an American is to mistake them for each other. The one who's offended is Canadian. There's more than apocryphal truth to this. People think hockey is Canada's national pastime, but what really brings the Great White North together is disapproval of the country next door. If the community of nations were middle school, Canada would be on safety patrol, courteous, eager, prissy. America would be the rich girl with big breasts and loose ways.

I flung off my orange safety vest one day, and went running after her.

I don't know exactly when my feelings deepened past infatuation, but I'll never forget noticing that they had. I was home for my father's funeral at the end of the summer of 2001. Patrick had returned stateside, ahead of me and the children, to get back to work. He called me one morning from his office. It was Tuesday.

"Are you watching TV?" he said. I wondered what juicy political or celebrity news had broken.

"The boys are watching something on CBC," I told him.

"Turn on an American channel. Two planes have crashed into the World Trade Center."

It was like the confounding of tongues in Babylon. I couldn't understand what he was saying. I grabbed onto the words that were the most familiar. *Plane crash*, I thought. *An accident*. But as I set the phone down and lunged for the living room, my mind was parsing the rest of the sentence. *Two planes. Two. Two is not an accident*.

I picked up the remote control and pressed an arrow. Not an accident. An attack. On my friends, on my neighbors, on my husband and my children. *This is what it means to be hated*. The TV screen a mirror held up to my heart, blown out and crumbling. I gathered my sons in my arms, realizing for the first time that they have mortal enemies because they are Americans.

I was due to return to Little Rock through Boston, our usual route. Now I was stranded, like everyone else; detained once more on the other side of the border from Patrick. While running errands one morning a few days after the attacks, I caught the live radio broadcast of ceremonies on Parliament Hill honoring those who had died. The Canadian anthem was played first. Then a Mountie sang "The Star-Spangled Banner." I laid my forehead on the wheel of my mother's car and wept with a heart that was truly broken. In that moment, it was no longer "their" anthem. It was mine, too.

Though I have sometimes, fleetingly, questioned the wisdom of it, I brought my children home to their country after September 11, 2001. I gave birth to another U.S. citizen. My sons are smart, healthy, and beloved. They are also white, middle-class, American males, which is to say they are princes—extraordinarily privileged, even in the shifting world order. The responsibility I feel for their upbringing is beyond personal for me. It's global. In them, I like to think I am helping to raise a new nation, one with fewer enemies, at home and abroad. Be kind, I tell them. Share. Take turns. Stand up for your brother. Include the girls. Use your words. Look after the little ones. Pick up after yourselves. Co-operate. And when you promise allegiance to the flag, remember what it stands for: liberty and justice for all people. I believe in those words. But my kids have never heard me pledge them.

My cold feet were easier to rationalize when becoming a U.S. citizen meant renouncing my Canadian citizenship. Nobody has ever blamed me for not wanting to sever ties with a country that offers universal health care and vacations in Cuba. But that excuse no longer holds water. The rules have changed, and it is possible for me to hold dual citizenship now. By virtue of their birth, my kids are already dual citizens.

"You're Canadians, too," I remind them occasionally. But they don't really know what that means, and I can't tell them, because I don't know, myself, except as a stance apart. I am Canadian mainly when I am exasperated with the United States and want to distance myself from its messes and its problems. I'm Canadian if I don't like the election results or I disagree with a war. I wear my Canadian identity like a T-shirt that says "Not with Stupid." I'm not sure I know what patriotism is, but I'm pretty sure that isn't it.

The childish truth is, I haven't wanted to commit. Becoming a U.S. citizen would mean having to dismount from my Royal Canadian high horse. It would mean having to say, "I'm an American," not just on a day when a black man is elected president, and I could burst with pride, but on days when U.S. missiles strike down children in another land, on days when the Stars and Stripes decorate a mob's hatred, on days when greed and piracy are sold as freedom. It would mean having to sing *my* country, 'tis of thee, in praise and in lament.

It would mean I belong.

I've gotten used to the idea of not belonging anywhere. It's romantic to play the exile, the desperado. But that's a thin veneer of bravado pasted over a lifetime of yearning. I used to think I could act, look, work, even marry my way into belonging, right up to the moment I'd realize that I hadn't, in the shattering way a bird comes face-to-face with its truth in a patio door. Epiphany of bone and glass.

I didn't realize that belonging isn't something you can make happen. It's something you let happen.

In Newfoundland, the old people say you are "in the fairy" when you are lost in a dream. All these years, there's been a part of me that believed I had wandered into the fairy, into this American dream, and that I would eventually wander back out. That my enchantment with this country was just that: an enchantment. In the back of my mind, there was a voice that kept saying, *Someday, I'll wake up and go home.*

The last time I crossed the border was through the Toronto airport, on my way back from a reading in Canada. I followed the moving sidewalks and escalators to the same U.S. Customs area as I did on that November day all those years ago, only now I got to stand in the line for U.S. citizens and alien residents. My hands and smile were steady as I passed my green card over the counter. The customs inspector smiled back, then frowned. In a post-traumatic flashback, an American bald eagle glared and flexed its talons.

"Do you know this is about to expire?"

Ignorance is no defense, I know, and I'm sure it sounded lame to say I'd forgotten that I wasn't a U.S. citizen, but it was the truth. I need to be reminded that I'm not a U.S. citizen, because the rest of the time, I feel American. I assured the customs inspector that I would update my immigrant status as soon as I got home, and boarded the plane.

For the last leg of my itinerary, I was on a tiny regional flight, bound from Chicago for Little Rock. There was no mistaking my fellow passengers for anything but Americans: across the aisle, a death row prison guard was flying home to an execution that night. Behind me, a born-again Christian was preaching to his seatmate. Ahead of me sat a large black woman, her hair sculpted and lacquered into a rigid, gleaming mass that never touched the headrest. They were all very different from me, but they felt very familiar. Not characters. People. My people.

The next day, I climbed to the attic to retrieve a box, then pulled out the file that held my old immigration records. I had already looked over the forms online and spoken with the consultant who had helped me with my green card application. Naturalization would be a lengthy and expensive process. It would be so easy to apply for a renewal instead. To buy myself another ten years of limbo, of wait-and-see.

A faded piece of facsimile paper was tucked among the visas and medical records. It was a poem from my father, faxed to me in Mexico, his way of blessing my departure from his country. Although at the time, I had assured him I'd come back to the island someday, it was clear that he had seen my path unfolding differently. *Going toward yourself is the longest journey of all,* he wrote. I could hear his priestly intonation in my mind, and was reminded of a line of Deuteronomy.

*These words shall be on your heart. You shall teach them to your sons and talk of them when you sit in your house, and when you walk, and when you lie down, and when you rise up.*

These are the words I should teach my sons. Going toward yourself is the longest journey of all. Belong.

The thermal ink of my father's signature had faded with time. Had it really been fourteen years since I came across the border? All around me were the dusty boxes full of files and memorabilia to prove it. *A long time wandering in the fairy,* I thought. *Time to wake up.* I climbed downstairs, went to my computer, and opened a file. N-400: Application to Become a U.S. Citizen. Under "Your Name" I began typing. Pittman, Kyran.

Time to come home.

17.

# The Crush

Though it might come as a surprise to some—including my husband—for all thirteen years of our marriage, I have been continuously and completely monogamous. I'm kind of surprised by it myself. I wouldn't blame anyone who wouldn't put it past me to cheat. For one thing, I am married to the man with whom I cheated on my first husband. For another, I don't play the part of reformed sinner very well. When stories of extramarital affairs come up, my friends are used to me withholding judgment. It's not that I think it's okay to sneak around. I just don't feel like I have a ticket to the stoning. In fact, I'm adamant that I am not the person anyone wants counseling them through a case of hot and bothered. Not if they're looking for someone else to put on the safety brake.

"Adultery kind of worked out for me," I tell them, with more honesty and less chagrin than is probably seemly. It did work out for me, but I'd hardly write it up as a prescription for anyone. It worked out in the sense that an organ transplant works out—with pain, risk, and scarring. Worse, I wasn't the only person to suffer the consequences. That much, I do regret. But I can't pretend that an affair is the worst thing that could ever happen to someone, or that a marriage is such a fragile orb, it pops the minute someone sticks a body part outside of it. Affairs change marriages—even the ones that go unconfessed and undiscovered—but those changes aren't always bad. A marriage might not survive them, but infidelity isn't like breaking a spell, where everything instantly goes "poof." Unless you've been living in a fairy tale, that is, in which case, something was going to burst your bubble eventually.

As for my husband, he's not the jealous type, but he assumes every man I meet is going to fall in love with me the way he did, and try to win me away the way he did.

"Honey, nobody else is that crazy," I tell him, and he has the good humor to agree. There's a subtext to our banter, though. We're depth sounding. *Are you worried? Should I be?*

My reassurances are never as direct or unequivocal as he would like. Words like "never" and "forever" feel glib to me; easy to say, and impossible to guarantee. Like the sober alcoholic who knows "never again" is a fool's pledge, I've kept my promise, for thirteen years, one day at a time. Not once, in all those years, have I so much as kissed another man.

But I have been untrue.

"Archer," he said, rising from his chair to extend a hand across the restaurant table. He was more handsome in person than in his profile photo. I like to place people's faces in time. His belonged to the nineteenth century. A gentleman farmer, I thought. Like Ashley Wilkes in *Gone With the Wind,* but absent of torment.

"Hey, so great you could come out," I said, before turning to tell the next person some variation on the same sentiment. I had business in the city, and had suggested a meet-up with some of my online friends in the area, mostly other writers, some of whom I'd met before, others whom I was meeting in person for the first time. Of all the people I was looking forward to seeing that night, his name was barely on my radar. We had connected through mutual friends and exchanged quips from time to time. I had noticed his wit, but had missed the charm. It was a pleasant surprise, but he was just one of several charming and witty dinner companions that night. It was all delicious.

But after it was over, and I was back in my hotel room, it was the thought of him that lingered, like the Turkish spice and incense that clung to my hair and clothes.

The thought lingered with me all the next day, and into the evening, when I took supper by myself in the bar and imagined him wandering in, us having a drink together by ourselves. It lingered through my flight home, and wafted around my head over the next few months—faintly, but pleasantly. His first message to me after our meeting made me think some thought of me lingered with him, too. Our online exchanges became more frequent, and frequently, more private. One day it came up that we both had plans to be out on our respective towns that night, with friends, and not spouses. We should text each other the play by play, we joked, with a semicolon wink. I gave him my mobile number, and we did. It was all very innocent. There was nothing in our messages I couldn't share with my husband. Yet I didn't.

I am good at keeping secrets, especially from myself.

We were becoming good friends, I thought. We should extend it to our mates. I bet I'd like your wife, I told him. You should visit, he said. We might, I replied.

"We should take a road trip this summer," I told Patrick. "I know lots of people we could stay with on the way."

There was a writers' conference I was going to first. My friend wondered if it was something he would find of interest.

YES, I texted. PLEASE come!

Well, that was a bit much, I thought, immediately after I sent it. *What's gotten into you?* I modified my encouragement with a nonchalant e-mail. It's a great conference, I wrote, as if the program was what had me so excited. There are lots of sessions you'd find interesting. By all means, come. If you want to.

*Please want to.*

He was there somewhere, in the crowd milling around the coffee urns. I stopped at the entrance and scanned. Where are you? I texted.

Here.

On one sudden, indrawn breath, the feeling that had wafted so airily around my consciousness for months filled the hollows of my skull and moved into my chest, as dense as smoke. It made me high.

"Let's take a walk," he said.

Dizzy, I nodded, and followed him into the bright sunshine, and we walked a few blocks to a pub. We ordered drinks, and he began talking about his marriage. He loved his wife, he said. He would never do anything to hurt his family. *Thank God.* Providence was going to save me from myself. Me too, I said. Me neither.

We went back out into the bright sunshine. It was all going to be fine. I could take in this giddy, high feeling, and breathe it out when I left. Nothing was going to happen. And nothing did, though we seemed to be at each other's side, or texting our way back there, for most of those forty-eight hours. On the last night of the conference, we gathered with other attendees in the lobby bar, amiably lounging side by side on a leather banquette. We were laughing and talking, and then it hit me.

"We're never going to see each other again," I said, too softly for anyone but him to hear. It wasn't a question, but he answered it anyway.

"Probably not," he said, looking at me over his old-fashioned glass as he raised it to his mouth. He lowered it and gave the ice cubes a swirl, watching them meditatively.

I was suddenly, miserably, homesick and tired. The party was over. People began to return to their rooms. I gave him the same hug and kiss on the cheek good night that I gave to everyone, and then he was gone. I went back to my room, and realized I had left my key card at the bar. It was nearly empty when I got there. A jacket had been left hanging over a chair. I picked it up. His, of course.

Well, fuck me. At least that's what it was going to look like when I knocked on his door. But I couldn't just leave it there. Sighing, I took the elevator up.

"You left this," I said, trying to be businesslike about it, when he answered the door. There was a snort, and a click behind us as his roommate locked us out in the hall together. He turned his reddened face to the door and knocked in mock desperation.

*You bastard,* I thought. Obviously, I had become the butt of a late-night fraternity joke. He turned around again to face me. *Say something,* I begged silently. *Say that we can't, but that you would, if we could. Say that you feel the same thing. Be gallant, at least.*

He looked at the carpet instead.

"Good night, Archer," I said, turning down the hall. "Good-bye."

I was the proverbial furious woman scorned. What had I been thinking, I asked myself, all the way home. He was a milquetoast, not half the man my husband was. Patrick, in fact, had never looked better. It was like waking up from a bad dream that causes you to cling to your beloved all day. I had been reckless, playing chicken with the edge, thinking I could jam on the brakes at the last minute. But would I have, if the corridor scene had played out differently? It was hard to say. What I felt that night was intensely physical, outside my brain's jurisdiction. It was heady, like the hot, alcohol note of freshly uncorked wine—the whiff of it invited a taste. To put it very simply, I was turned on. And it wasn't that easy to turn off. In fact, I didn't want to turn it off. For the short duration of my crush, I felt sexier than I had in a long time. I had more sex than I'd had in a long time, with my husband, and not as a stand-in, but starring as himself. My on/off switch is a toggle, not a dial. It may have been someone else that tripped the switch, but once it was on, it was *on*.

It had all been delectable. Until I scared myself. I had probably scared Archer, too. As the days passed, and my fury burned down to less hellish proportion, I found sympathy for him. He did what he had to do to protect his family, and who could fault him for that? It was how I'd want Patrick to act in the face of some other woman's weak moment. I thought about his wife. From what I could tell, I might have liked her. And even if I didn't, I certainly wouldn't wish to cause her harm. There was a time, when I was much younger, when I considered a lover's marital status to be his concern, not mine. But I wasn't that girl anymore; hadn't been in a long time. Staying married is hard enough when there are only two people involved. Over and above fidelity to my husband, I owe an allegiance to other wives and mothers. And other daughters.

I was just shy of sixteen when I was first confronted with undeniable evidence of my father's infidelity. A couple of lines of type, on a white piece of paper rolled around the cylinder of his typewriter at the dining room table. The salutation caught my eye. A woman's name. I didn't have to turn the knob to see it was a love letter. In an instant, I knew all that I already knew. There was an underlying order to all the chaos: the bitter arguments in the middle of the night, my mother crying in the bathroom, the sudden separations and reconciliations. It wasn't random after all. I was almost relieved.

Later I learned of other women: some whom I knew well,

others who were peripherally familiar to me, pretty faces hovering at the edge of a memory, a foreign accent when I picked up the phone. Some were brief, but none were casual. My father was not a casual man. I think he loved all of them. When I told him I was leaving my first husband for Patrick, he acknowledged there had been affairs, and that he regretted only one—the one that ended his marriage to my mother. He was honestly surprised when she finally divorced him.

I knew that my father's unfaithfulness hurt my mother, but I never really considered how it hurt me. I had always identified with the cheater or the mistress, and I had played both roles. I never saw myself in my mom's shoes until I got old enough to line my feet up next to hers. As we passed our tenth anniversary, and I approached forty, marriages started coming apart all around us. A few weeks after I came home from the conference, I stood in a dark parking lot outside a restaurant, letting the latest casualty notification sink in. Patrick was twenty feet away, saying good night to one of the people we'd just come from dinner with, white ash drifting from the end of his cigarette as he gestured. I looked at my girlfriend.

"My God," I said. "How awful."

She nodded. "I've heard he's already moved out and is living with the new woman."

"Jesus."

We kept our voices low, more out of solemnity than secrecy. If we had been ten or fifteen years younger, such news would have been gossip. Pretty, young things can go whistling past the graveyards of other women's marriages. At our age, we all but crossed ourselves. I wished we were truly alone, and I could confess my summer crush in depth. Instead, I gave her the abstract.

"Sometimes I feel like I should run out and have an affair, now, just because," I said. "Because what if I want to later and I can't, because nobody wants me anymore? What if it turns out we squandered all of our youth on men who go and leave us later for younger women?"

*What if they are all like my father?*

Relaying the news to Patrick on the ride home in the car, my voice turned to thick liquid, pooling in the back of my throat. I again felt the urge to confess everything. But I didn't have it in me to do the necessary reassuring. I was too badly in need of that myself. I thought I would start to cry.

"You don't understand what it's like for a woman to get older. Your currency will just go up, while mine goes down. You don't know how that feels, how scary it is to think you'll become invisible. How it feels like you're running out of something you'll never get back."

He let me carry on in the key of "You don't" for about half the drive. Then he spoke, in the low and quiet tone he uses only when he really needs me to shut up and hear something.

"You listen to me," he said. "You were the most beautiful woman I had ever seen when you were twenty-five. You are the most beautiful woman I have ever seen now. If I live that long, you will be the most beautiful woman I will ever see when you are eighty. You will always be the most beautiful woman in the world to me, because you are the *only* woman in the world for me. And nothing will ever change that."

I looked at the man who had told me those very same words

on the day we met. The man who repeated them every time after, when I told him again and again it was over and sent him away. The man who traveled for seven days on Greyhound buses through the worst blizzard of the century, for over 2,500 miles, with no reason to believe that I would keep my word to meet him at the last station, only an abiding belief in his own word. Those words. This man. The One.

What was there to confess that was not already seen and understood? I felt known, seen, and loved. Everything else was incidental.

That summer bolted like a neglected garden. Early one morning in August, I walked around the yard to assess just how far it had gotten away from me. Trumpet vine had taken over the dog fence. The fig tree was turning yellow, and the birds were beating us to the ripened fruit I thought we would be devouring all season. The dogwoods and forsythia were wizened with thirst, beggars in my path. The children were wild. During the day, I'd catch glimpses of them through the hedges, brown skinned, running half naked with handfuls of hard green pecans and tall pointed sticks. Everywhere, there were hidden caches of sticks, rocks, and nuts. Provision or ammunition, I couldn't tell. I had let it all go, myself included, and it had been the most luscious, rambling summer in years.

But it was time. Time to pull back the lovely tangle of vines before they choked the life out of something, time to beg forgiveness from the dogwoods and forsythia so they would love me again in the spring, time to brood even one fig into full sweetness. Time to give Peter his thimble and gather in my lost boys.

I nursed my indignation over Archer for a little while longer. It made me feel like less of a fool, and filled the space where my crush had been. I didn't miss him, but I would miss that. There's a trade-off for being happily long-married. The energy of anticipation diminishes, just like collagen or pigment. You can simulate it, but it's not the same. There are no more first kisses. But there is deeper intimacy, and paradoxically, there is more mystery. In the early years of our relationship, we had to know everything the other thought, felt, did. Every issue had to be exposed, examined, and resolved, immediately. It was like living in the nude. Sexy for a while, but eventually too familiar. Our second decade feels more spacious, as if we've moved into a different house, where the doors are left open, but there is room to retreat, rest, and change, without anyone having to sneak out a window. So far, I like it, though if I thought my husband was texting flirtatious messages to another woman from one of his rooms, I might start knocking holes in walls.

"You don't have to worry about me," I tease him when we do our depth sounding, and he accuses me—rightly—of a double standard when it comes to being nosy. "I know what *I'm* up to."

But I don't always know what I'm up to, any more than I can really know what's happening with him. I was right about his currency going up. He grows more attractive, more confident, more interesting every year. I'm unlikely to be the only woman who takes note of it. I'm unlikely to be the youngest or the prettiest. I don't think I need to know. I'm fairly sure I don't want to know. I'd rather just trust him. If I can survive the occasional bout of wanderlust and temptation, he surely can. If he gets a little lost while daydreaming down the path not taken, I have to believe he'll find his way back, like I did.

There is, in every woman I know, a creature that cannot be domesticated. It prowls through our dreams, enters the house, casts cold eyes on our mate and children, and holds us rapt in its terrible beauty. You can love your husband and children with every breath in your body and still feel restless and detached sometimes. You can be a good mother, and have daydreams of running, or simply walking, away. It's the ones who can't accept this paradox who have the most to fear, are most vulnerable to the sudden ambush of desire.

My favorite maritime legend is the story of the seal wife, trapped in human form by a love-struck fisherman who steals her pelt. They marry, have children, and she lives happily ever after on two legs, until one morning she finds her hidden skin, and remembers herself. She puts it on, and goes home. Just like that. No hand-wringing, no good-bye note, no dropping off the kids with the neighbor. Some mornings I step outside in my red satin robe to pick up the newspaper, and gaze down the length of the driveway, past the minivan, bikes, and soccer balls, to the street beyond. I picture her walking down to the sea. A whisper of satin, a splash, and she's gone. Her red robe at the water's edge, the newspaper still rolled.

We belong completely to the lives we've made. And still, not at all.

I've heard from my old crush a few times since the bonfire of my vanity died down. Brief and probably impulsive updates to let me know all is well with him and his family. I don't think of him much in between, but when I do, I still see him as the gentleman farmer, cultivating his garden, maintaining good fences. It makes me happy to know I didn't trample it. I can't imagine what would have attracted me to such a tidy and careful person in the first place, except maybe our own garden needed a little tending. Years ago, we listened to some marriage enrichment lectures that suggested married crushes can be used as diagnostics, pointing to some characteristic that is deficient within the marriage. I decided to test it on my husband's admitted object of extramarital fantasy, a temp receptionist at his office.

"What's she like?" I asked, open to learning where we needed to shore things up.

"Blond," he said, without hesitating. "Dumb as a post."

At the time, I was heavily immersed in Jungian studies. Every aspect of our lives, waking and dreaming, was wrung out for hidden meaning. Obviously, I needed to lighten up.

In recent years, I've watched married friends of mine ride out their own crushes, from mild to severe. It must be our age. It's like the dance of the mayflies, with everybody's libido at two minutes to midnight. Most of these are passing fancies, the kind that afflict almost everybody at some point over the course of a long-term relationship, me included. "Just put your head between your knees and breathe deeply a few times," I told one friend. "You'll be all right." She was all right. But she never looked more beautiful than she did those few weeks. I could almost smell the electrical charge in the air around her. Something in her was wide awake, and I was the last person to tell her to hit the snooze button. Every married person has to grapple with temptation in their own way, run their own cost-benefit analysis to come up with the reasons why or why not. Me, I've done the affair. I pulled the chute cord. I know where it lands you.

It lands you back in a relationship, is where. A relationship strewn with the inevitable tedium, crankiness, and wanderlust that accompany two people living together, no matter how much they love each other. You don't need to have fundamental compatibility issues; those weeds can sprout from trivial ones. Like the time we went to the new pizza place in town. Within moments of arriving, it was clear that Patrick was less than thrilled about the place. It was crowded and busy when we got there, the service was rushed, the food was expensive, and customers were swarming for tables. It was a kind of hive atmosphere, because this is a small town, and the place was getting lots of buzz. My husband is particularly resistant to social buzz. I could tell it was grating on him like the noise of fluorescent lights.

Me, I was excitedly flitting around. I love buzz. I thought it felt festive. The restaurant's specialty was wood-fired pizza, served up in a style I would call "rustic," and my husband called "sloppy." We ordered, and when our pies arrived, with their toppings in a more or less virgin state (slices of cheese instead of shredded, fresh baby spinach instead of cooked), I was the only one smiling.

We argued about it all the way home, and well into the next week.

"That place was awful," said Patrick, "sloppily prepared food and no service masquerading as philosophy."

"It's trying to do something different and creative," I said.

"Pretentious," he declared. "Inflated."

"Small-minded," I charged. "Judgmental."

We were moving beyond critiquing the food, and into one of

our dirtier forms of fighting, spinning a disagreement into evidence of each other's "issues." The negative side of being even a little bit hip to psychology, which we are, is that you can use it as a handy weapon in a pinch.

Clearly, I told Patrick, he was threatened by the pizza's success.

Our hot air was a bellows to the embers of another disagreement we'd had a few weeks before, when Patrick decided he needed to shade all the windows in his beautiful sunlit office in order to see his work on his computer screen. Sunlight to me is like oxygen. The idea that the windows in that room, in the center of the house, would be permanently shaded, made me crazy. Worse, I knew I didn't have a leg to stand on: He's the one who has to work there, and he let me have my way in virtually every other aspect of interior decoration. All I could do was sulk. And glower. Which is what I did every time I passed through his office for the next two days, thinking, go ahead, take a happy, bright space and make it a sad and dark space. *Like your soul.*

Because natural light is important to me, and if it's not as important to him, then he must be wrong. And bad. And most likely a fascist. And if he doesn't like his very expensive pizza flung down in front of him with all the toppings scattered unevenly and the edges a little charred from the wood fire, if he didn't find that charming, if he didn't *get that,* he must not get me.

I know better than to nurse that line of thinking at my bosom for very long. It's temptation, waiting to strike, with the lie that I would be infinitely happier with someone *different*. Something new. It promises that somewhere out there is a man who loves full-spectrum light and artisanal cuisine as much as I do, and I owe it to myself to find him, and spend the rest of my life with him under the Tuscan sun, eating wood-fired pizza alfresco, in the nude. But different and new is just the same old if you keep doing it over and over. The real novelty for me lies in seeing what the next decade of marriage brings.

What I've taken from the first is this: If you can hang in there through minor and major differences of opinion, through each other's big and little fuck-ups, year after year, you come to understand that the person you married is really, terribly flawed. There isn't a human being you can hang out with, day in and day out, for over a decade, and not come to the same inescapable realization. You can find a new lover who gets you and completes you, and you can run off together and never look back. One day, *I promise,* you will find yourself leaving a restaurant with that very person, wondering what in the world you are doing with someone so obviously wrong for you in every way. But in that same instant, in a one-two punch to your consciousness, you'll realize he has wondered the very same thing about you; that the real wonder is that any two people stay together, as impossible to live with and as broken as we all are.

# 18

# Good-bye, Girl

The dress is one hundred percent pure vintage polyester. The fabric is flimsy and printed with a psychedelic shooting star motif, in faded rainbow colors. It has long flared sleeves and a halter-style top with a keyhole opening at the bosom. The hemline barely skirts public decency. I always wore it with five-inch stiletto heels. Patrick audibly panted whenever I put it on. He said it was a dress a Marvel comic book artist would draw on a girl, a fantasy straight out of his seventies boyhood. He called it the Super Heroine Dress. I'd sling my fringed leather jacket over it and go out to make the scene.

To make *a* scene, more accurately. Musicians onstage missed notes when I walked into a club wearing that outfit. Conversations stopped. Women whispered and men stared. I saved it for special occasions, as if wearing it was a kind of gift I brought.

I wore it to birthday celebrations. To gigs and concerts. To the funeral of an old hippie friend, accessorized with a matching rainbow bouquet of helium balloons, which I released to the blue sky when his ashes were scattered.

It was outrageous. I was outrageous.

Then I became a mom. As my body and my lifestyle changed, an identity crisis came to lurk in my closet.

"I don't know who this girl is," I lamented from deep inside it one day, clutching the phone in one hand, a silver lamé halter in the other. I'd called a friend in a panic attack brought on by an attempted wardrobe purge. "I don't know where she fits anymore."

It made sense to let go of the shiny cropped tops and the low-slung pants, the crazy shoes and the short-shorts. When I got pregnant, I took my belly button ring out and let the piercing grow over. Those were all appropriate edits. I couldn't chase toddlers around the playground in Lucite stripper shoes. It wasn't as if I was expunging sexiness from my life, succumbing to the mom haircut and mom jeans. But the excisions weren't painless either. Whenever I came to the Super Heroine Dress, the purge was over. I could never part with it, but neither could I imagine wearing it. I would close the closet door, unable to reconcile that wild child with motherhood and maturity.

I tried. On a whim, I put a customized license plate on my minivan that was imprinted with the words HIPMAMA. It was meant as a personal affirmation, but it soon felt like false advertising. There was no way I could consistently deliver on it, unless you interpreted the term to mean a woman whose offspring are attached to her hip, or a reference to anatomical changes wrought by childbirth. After we downsized to one vehicle, Patrick found the license plate equally hard to live up to, and I was just as glad to remove it. I thought I'd get a tattoo instead, something artful and discreet—a more private reminder that, beneath the capri pants and nursing tops, I still rocked it. I had my design picked out and was ready to go when I discovered I was pregnant again.

"I guess you got tattooed all right," a friend smirked.

Surrender, the universe seemed to be saying. You're not That Girl anymore.

Oh, but I loved being That Girl. I knew exactly how to be her. I understudied for years as a kid, playing with Barbie dolls and reading fashion and beauty magazines. I practiced dress-up more than I ever rehearsed being a mommy. As an awkward-looking preteen, I despaired of ever getting to be her. As an insecure teenager, I faked that I was her. As a young newlywed playing house with my first husband, I buried her. And then I came to America, anonymous and free, and I became her.

"Like a movie stah," one of our neighbors used to say, every time he saw me in one of my getups. "Like a seventies homecoming queen," said Danny, the cook at the bar one day, looking me up and down, as I sauntered past in my standard waitressing uniform, bell-bottom jeans, towering heels, and a bared midriff. "Where *did* you come from?"

I laughed with the sheer pleasure of having created something that someone else appreciated. From nowhere, I told him. I made myself up.

Of course, I couldn't really pass for a movie star or homecoming queen, or even the prettiest girl in that barroom or most others. It was always a game of dress-up, closer to drag than fashion. But when I wore those clothes, I felt like a beautiful girl, enough to convince others that I was, or at least convince them to play along with me. It was a wonderful time, and there was a part of me that was sad to leave the ball when the clock struck midnight and turned my belly into a pumpkin. Any illusions I might have had about staying sexy through pregnancy, like real movie stars and prom queens do, were banished the first time I looked down and saw that there was a coffee ring on my maternity shirt, a few inches above the spot where I once sported a belly button ring. My girth was enormous enough for me to have rested my mug on it, level, while sitting up. I think of it as The Day Sexy Died.

It was later revived, but it's never been the same. Fortunately, becoming a mother puts sexiness in perspective. As does turning forty. It's not that it doesn't matter, it's that a lot of other things matter more. I wouldn't trade who I am now to be able to wear hot pants and thigh-high boots again. But it would be a lie to say I have been cheerfully letting go. As evolved as it would sound to claim that I embrace the first wiry gray hairs, the crow's-feet, and stretch marks as badges of experience, the truth is less pure. I mourn a little inside when I see a photograph of me with long glossy tresses and taut belly.

I've heard older women say that sometimes when they look in the mirror, they don't feel like themselves anymore. The image no longer reflects how they feel inside. A friend of mine in her sixties recently had a face-lift. Although we are close, there was a note of hesitation when she told me her plans. I think she was afraid I would judge.

When I was younger, I would have. There are all kinds of objections to be made to excising age this way, as if it were malignant. I always feel a little betrayed when I discover that someone who is older and beautiful has had "work" done. Because until I've learned the truth, I think perhaps it's possible for me to age as beautifully. *Look at her,* I think. *Fifty, and still so sexy. Well, why not? Maybe I could be, too. Who's afraid of fifty? Not me.* And then I find out they've "cheated," and I despair a little.

My friend is as smart, as strong, and as deep as anyone I know. I couldn't judge her decision. If ridding myself of ten pounds or neck wrinkles were as easy as plucking gray hairs, what would the difference be? If I can have my hair cut or colored so that I feel my best, why not alter my face or my breasts? I use a face cream that removes old skin cells. Could I use a laser to remove more? A scalpel? Where is the line? I thought I knew it when I was thirty. Now I'm less sure.

I miss making heads turn. I am trying to accept that I will never weigh less than 120 pounds again without acute deprivation. It irritates me that the makeup and hair styling I used to do for fun now feels as necessary a prerequisite to leaving the house as brushing my teeth. It takes work just to look *okay* to myself. The big guns, like self-tanner and Lycra, are no longer just for special occasions. So much that was once optional and playful has become a maintenance chore. There's a striving to it that feels familiar, like those insecure teenage years, when I was trying so hard to act my way into someone I didn't know how to be yet.

I flicked on my straightening iron the other morning, and realized that the daily use of hair appliances is something I haven't done since I was a teenager, when I would set my radio alarm clock for five in the morning so I could scorch and lacquer my layered hair into sausage curls before school. In those years I wore a mask—literally—made with thick coats of cheap makeup. I used to wince to see old photos in which my face would be an entirely different flesh tone than my neck, but I came to look more lovingly upon them later. In some ways, the mask protected me while I was in that tender, larval state. It came off when I was ready to take it off and become my shiny new self.

I looked around my bathroom, noticing that every shelf and drawer was filled with the latest potions and powders, and realized I am back in metamorphosis again, straining toward what I don't yet know how to be. I understudy older women as carefully as I once pored over those beauty magazines, taking note of what works and doesn't work; dress, hair, makeup, comportment. Taking note of who has aged gracefully, who has hung on to her younger persona well past time, or who seems to have abandoned any interest in her own appearance. I especially note who can command respect and attention when she speaks, because so many older women often seem invisible and powerless in the company of men.

I'm embarrassed to admit that part has worried me. It seems ridiculously regressive that twenty years after adolescence, I am back to wondering how to get the boys to take notice, but the easy, obvious answer is getting less easy and obvious. Youthful sex appeal is a hefty talking stick in our culture. When it passes from me, will my voice still be heard? Maybe in ten or twenty years, I'll laugh at that question, and look back with fond bemusement at photos of my bottle-tanned, Lycra-bound forties. Maybe I won't miss being That Girl, because by then, I'll have become That Woman.

I actively scan the horizon for women who personify her with their vitality. I have one arm stretched out to them, and I am trying to summon the courage to let go with the other, make the leap, and grab hold of my future with energy and determination rather than just passively losing my grasp on the old power base. I swing back and forth on this trapeze, working my way up to flying across the gap, into the unknown.

I decided I would give myself a push by retiring the Super Heroine Dress in style. I wore it out dancing with friends one night, made the scene with it one more time. The polyester-draped figure I cut was that of a middle-aged mother of three, not a twenty-five-year-old party girl. Definitely not from the panel of a Marvel comic book. Definitely not the fantasy of any teenage boy.

I think it's okay. I have given birth to three children. I am a good mother. I've made it to the second decade of a marriage. I have many friends, a career that I love. I have different strengths now. I tell myself it is going to be okay. Better than okay.

As a friend in her fifties assures me, there are some pretty great compensations for not being the center of attention with the guys anymore. One of those, I'm discovering, is finally finding my place among women. I have somehow always had great girlfriends, but for years, I had no clue how to be one. My closest female friendships always came behind even the most casual relationship with a man. Women were Plan B. I could never have imagined, when I was twenty-five, being so content to spend an entire evening with only them, let alone looking forward to it all week.

My innermost circle of girlfriends widens, contracts, and rotates, with axis coordinates that change with the seasons. But for a few weeks in the spring they are fixed: five o'clock sharp, my front porch, kids welcome, no husbands, no regrets. The drinks are fancy, the snack is simple. The children are encouraged to play video games and forage from the pantry. It's our time. The Ladies have convened.

We talk about hair and makeup, sex, clothes, religion, music, food, and the riddle of being wives and mothers, and still ourselves. The laughter becomes deep and earthy. The second round is shaken and poured. Someone puts chicken nuggets in the microwave for the children. The husbands are called, soothed, cajoled, notified. A little while longer.

Patrick stays discreetly in the background, steering our boys toward baths and homework. On a trip inside to refill the ice bucket, I tease him, "We are talking about our vaginas. You don't want to go out there!" He raises his eyebrows in mock horror, smiles.

When the kids slip outside, hovering near the porch like moths around lamplight, I wonder if I should shoo them back inside, if our conversation is too strong for them. Patrick herds them into the house, again and again, but they keep escaping, dancing on the lawn in the twilight, pagans around a mighty bonfire.

A twenty-five-year-old girl might be hot as hell. But she can't know that deep warmth, that fierce heat.

When I took the dress off for the last time and hung it back in the closet for keeps, I wasn't confused about why I would never let it go and why I didn't need to put it on again. I've kept it to honor that part of me who will always be a wild child, a beautiful girl. I don't need to wear it on the outside, because I'm cultivating its power on the inside.

It works differently that way. It may not command a room to full attention. It's lost altogether on some. But it's a power that's earned and owned in full, and time can't steal it away from me. Fade- and wrinkle-proof, one hundred percent genuine and pure.

# Cat's Cradle

In the daily stream of pouring milk, wiping noses, signing schoolwork, and the endless karmic cycle of loading and unloading the dishwasher, it's easy to think this is how my life has always been, and must always be. Memories of life before Patrick and the children seem like fragments of a dream to me now, or stories overheard in passing about someone else. But this time is measured, a length of string that's woven in and out of days like a nest built in my hands—elaborate but finite. My own mother is a reminder of that. She lives by herself now, in a different house from the one she shared with my father before he died, when my sister and I were their little girls. The structure of our life together as a family—so intricate, so permanent-seeming—collapsed between her hands when that time was done.

My boys are six, nine, and eleven. A band of changelings has taken the babies they were, and hidden them in a briar of limbs, freckles, and missing teeth. Milestones skip across the surface of their days so fast I miss them, and they have to call them out to me. "Mom! I jumped off the diving board!" "Mom! My tooth came out!"

But that tooth just came in, I think. And how long was he in the deep end?

"Mom!"

They can't conceive of a time or a place that didn't include them. Their consciousness is like a pre-Columbian map of the world, centered on themselves. Here in the middle of everything, are they. Somewhere, sketched amorphously in the margins of their awareness, is my life before them. I locate it for them on maps: up there, a ragged granite triangle in the North Atlantic, Newfoundland. That's where I was then. Down here, one roughly rectangular patchwork piece among four dozen, is where we live now. They can see it is a long route—about three thousand miles—but it looks relatively direct on paper. A strand of dots and numbered shields, broken by a few millimeters of blue; one very long day on planes when we travel to visit their cousins and grandmother. But that's not how their father came to me. I guide their fingers along his path, the last-ditch trek from Mexico to Newfoundland in winter, by land and sea. You go this way until you come to the end of everything. Then you go a leap further.

It's a leap of faith, I tell them in my heart. When you come to it, take it.

At the foot of our bed, there are stacked three antique suitcases. In the bottom one, at the oldest stratum of memorabilia, are reams of printed e-mails, bundled envelopes postmarked Mexico, United States, and Canada, the stubs of boarding passes and bus tickets, immigration visas, and maps. The artifacts of letting go. The middle contains baby curls and teeth, pressed flowers, yellowed obituaries, and old family photos—these are about hanging on. The top one still has room for keepsakes yet to come.

This is the layered archaeology of a small civilization: its origin myth and its sacred objects. It tells the story of a family. About becoming *us*, the construct we pass hand to hand, one generation to the next. But nested within our collective story, there is also my story, a story about what it means to belong: to a family and a place, and still, to oneself. The cat in the cradle. I would pass that to my children, too.

Oh, my sons, my lovely barbarians. See this string around my hands. Reach in. Hold on.

# ACKNOWLEDGMENTS

I wish to thank Laura Mathews, literary editor at *Good House-keeping*, for pulling my needle out of a haystack 500 million blogs high. Without her keen eye, deft hand, and extraordinary patience in unraveling the tangled threads that run through my wild mind, I would have no cause to thank my impeccable agent, Sally Wofford-Girand, or my wonderfully intuitive editor at River-head, Sarah McGrath. Together they have been midwives, cheer-leaders, and author-whisperers. My dream team.

A big thank-you to all my virtual frontier neighbors, the "mommy" and "daddy" bloggers—many now authors themselves—who have been so generous with their moral support, tactical advice, and diversionary wit. I am indebted to my loyal online read-ers, who incubated many of these stories with their kind attention, and whose e-mails and comments nourished and sustained me as I found my voice. Thank you for wandering over to visit, coffee in hand, day after day.

To my relatives and friends who cast a net of love and kindness over me from one corner of the world to another, and never let it go, in spite of being neglected, stood up, and repeatedly let down, I thank you for your support, and I beg your forgiveness. My beloved Little Rock girlfriends, who've heard most of these stories before, were the compass point as I wrote them. If I couldn't hear myself share the words over Thursday cocktails on my front porch, they didn't make it into the manuscript. Thanks for keeping me true.

To my sister, Emily, and my mother, Marilee, for standing by with outward calm and confidence while I rifled through our most personal family history. Thank you for your belief and trust. Forgive me my trespasses.

To my late father, the poet Al Pittman, I owe innumerable gifts, including one that is difficult for a parent to give a child: freedom. I hope to pass it to my sons, along with my love, my gratitude, and, as the child of a writer, my empathy for all that is wonderful and terrible about having a parent who turns life into books.

Finally, for Patrick, a quotation from *Joe Versus the Volcano,* one of my favorite cinematic fables:

"Thank you for my life. I forgot how *big.*"

Thank you.